Death Comes With No Choice

* * * * *

Non Fiction

By Award-Winning Author

By Pam McCagh

All my books were written through

Memories, Their Memories

My books will tell you all you need to know about life and Death and everything in between. They will connect you to your loved ones and tell their story.

You will learn about the weepers, the souls that never rest. You will understand reincarnation, as well as how, why, and when. But most of all, you will know The Truth, The Whole Truth and Nothing But the truth From The spirit people themselves.

Souls that have not found their resting place. They are known as the weepers.

They are called the weepers for a reason. Their souls have been dammed to live the existence of misery. And will never be allowed to return.

COPYRIGHT

CW01501736

The Copyrights of Pamela McCag

To be identified as the author of
by her in accordance with the (
Act.

This Is The Truth, The Whole, And Nothing But The Truth. I have honestly been there, and I was told to go back by the angel Of Mercy and that my life would change within two years.

It did change, and I kept my promise, and they kept theirs. I promised to listen to people from the other side telling me their stories of their life and Death experiences.

If you have crossed over and been given a second chance at life, I believe it was for a reason. Mine was listening to the other side's stories to help people understand. Not only life But also Death. I was a person of no belief, But I came back with a miracle of understanding both worlds.

Table of Contents

1.   Death Comes with No Choice

I was brought up to believe that when death comes, it comes with no choices, but since then, I have been involved with a different kind of death.

I believe that there are different ways to accept death. Nobody wants to die, but we do have a choice: when death calls - do we go or do we stay? It is up to us.

I am a firm believer that if you do not want to leave this world, you have the choice to stay. It is not a bad thing, in fact, because you can choose to stay, you are still able to select the things that you would like to do while you are here.

I have met some wonderful people who chose to stay. The Milkman was my first one, but there have been many more since. People talk about spooky things, but there is nothing spooky, not in the real world of death.

Most of the time, our loved ones are trying to communicate with us. I suppose you can say that I deal with the people who choose to stay. Once your loved ones have passed on, there is no need for us to stay here any longer.

People ask me all the time, "Where is the other side?" When we say the 'other side', what does it mean? It is not a place that is up or down or back or forward or the other side of things; it is a place of contentment of all things.

It is not a place we can see but a place we can feel. To those who have crossed over, it is a memory within a memory of their energies of life.

Until they have lost all thought of returning to the earth and accepted it, it is merely the beginning of a new entry into a new destination. I have read so many books about the spiritual world that sometimes you can get confused, so now I ask my guides, and they tell me to listen to my soul.

The ones who wait have asked me to tell their stories about themselves, their life, death and of the need to be among us once more - to belong once more but this time to let go of all the world's promises of all things here and forgotten. I have loved every moment of them being here with me and telling me their stories;

There are so many who still need to be heard. I hope that we will all meet again one day. The question is, when we die, do we go, or do we stay? I have met some wonderful spirits since I have been writing, and I have never found a story that has any malice whatsoever.

A long time ago, I learned about connecting to the other side. I used different methods before I learned that all you have to do is let go and accept. It is a wavelength of an energy force. It was a wonderful journey, and I am so grateful that they took me along on the ride.

This book is different from the other three. I have tried to keep each book different. The first one, Sleep Never Comes, was all about the spirit world and its stories. The second one, Can Butterflies Cry, was about beautiful memories, including mine. The fourth, well, you be the judge. I am just their storyteller.

2. A Stranger by My Side

Most of us, when we die, cross over quickly, but if we feel we want to stay and then stay, we will. We are reluctant to let go of something we know, love, or fear.

These two things keep us here: the people we have come to love or the places we have come to love and do not wish to leave like the young gentleman, who, for the first time, found something to love. It was not a person. It was an old house - but it was his house.

Then, there are the people who are too afraid to leave because they feel safe here on earth and do not wish to go somewhere they do not recognise or are just afraid to move on.

Then there is the story about a woman who had strong beliefs that it was her fault that her children died. It is the worst thing that I have ever known.

The loss of a child keeps us here. Guilt wraps around us like a tomb - it buries us within. I have met people who were so engrossed with guilt that it took them years to ask for help. Let me rephrase that: they do not ask for help until I pick up their energy, which is trapped between the two worlds.

It is like tuning into the radio but just cannot get that frequency right; no matter which way you turn, you just cannot connect to the person who is searching for that one type of connection.

When I feel it, or should I say, sense it, it is similar to a radio frequency. I search with my thoughts and mind for that wavelength, and then when I find it, I have to wait for that one split second before we both connect.

The phrase I like to use is 'reaching out' to each other. It is like a feeling of finding something at last.

When you find it, there is a sense of relief - that is the only way I can explain it: feeling, listening and holding on until that one last connection of letting go, of all the last thoughts of pain or guilt.

That is when everything comes together. It is like a thousand violins playing at once; it is like seeing the Sunshine for the first time; it is like being in the rain and feeling it on your face; it is like the greatest love of all. To hold on for all eternity is the final act of letting go and crossing over.

3.   This is her story.

Pass me the paper." She repeated again, "Could you please pass the paper?" Her voice was louder now. I turned and looked at her. *Could she see me?* I passed her the paper without taking my eyes off her. I then watched as she opened the paper and turned each page. She stopped and looked at me. "Did you say something?" she asked. I could not believe it - *could she really see me?*

I smiled, laughed, and cried all at the same time, and then I felt quite embarrassed. I reached out to touch her, to tell her I was so grateful to find someone who, at last, could see me, but my hand went straight through her arm. She looked at me strangely; I didn't know what to do. I reached out again, and once again, my hand went straight through.   She looked down at me through her glasses.

She said, "You don't have to worry none, as I can see you and hear you."

The only word that came out of my mouth was, "How?" She slowly folded the paper, placed it carefully on the bench and looked at me, then said that she had been waiting a long time for me to ask the question - *can you see me?*

I just did not know what to do. The stranger seemed to know what I was thinking. She touched my arm gently, and I was astonished that I could actually feel her touching my arm. *How can this be?* The stranger said, "Do not worry, I will explain later." In the same breath, she asked, "Would you like to walk with me now?"

I stood up automatically and started to walk for what seemed like hours without saying a word, but I knew what she was saying without words passing our lips. She asked, "What can you remember?"

I told her, "Nothing." Once again, she asked me without her lips moving. "What can you remember?" I looked at her blankly and replied quite sharply, "Nothing." We walked on again, not saying anything until we came to a huge tree. She beckoned me to sit down, and she sat across from me and just stared. My mind was trying not to panic. *What did this strange person want with me? Why does she keep asking about my memory?*

For the first time, I started to concentrate, trying so hard to remember. I looked across and shouted at her, "What am I supposed to remember?" Then something odd struck me - why was it when I reached out and touched the woman that my fingers went straight through her, and yet when she touched me, I could feel her touch? God help me! What was going on?

The woman came across, took me in her arms and said, "Shush now, everything is going to be ok."

I do not know why, but tears came streaming down my cheeks, and I could not stop myself from crying. I did not know what I was crying for.

Why is the woman here? What am I supposed to remember? As she gently rocked me from side to side, the pain and heartache started to slip away.

I could see myself in a huge field with children around me; I could feel the sun on my face and the happiness in my heart; I could hear the children calling "Mommy" as we all danced in the field together.

I heard Mother calling us for lunch. We always had the triangle on the porch, and Mother would come out with a steel rod and clunk on it. We knew it was time to come home for tea.

The sun was just going down as I watched the children running in front of me. I could hear the train coming over the crossing, making its usual noise, warning people not to cross.

I could hear the children still laughing, and then fear took over me. I shouted at them, but they laughed and screamed so loud they could not hear me. I ran, but before I knew what had happened, I saw my three children on the railway line.

My God, what happened? I do not remember anything. After that, the funerals came and went. I was not ready to accept anything. How could life be so cruel? Mother tried everything to comfort me, but all I could remember was their little bodies lying there lifeless.

From then on, I just slowly died. I blamed myself for taking them to the fields that day. I was back now, looking at the stranger who was still holding me. I asked, "Why? Why would you want to bring back the memories - the memories that I have suppressed all these years? Why?"

I kept asking her, but she just held me and said, "It's time to go now." "Go where?" I asked.

There is no way I want to go. She said, "Wouldn't you like to see your children again?" I thought, *how cruel could this person be?* She said, "Your children are waiting for you".

I could not believe what she was saying, so I opened my eyes and asked again, "Where?" She told me to take a deep breath and look. I asked, "Look for what?" She said, "Your children". I did not question her anymore.

I just looked, and yes, she was right. Coming towards me were my children with their arms outstretched, calling, "Mommy, we missed you".

4.   The Locket

Can you wish for something and wait all of your life, and then when you do get it, do you wonder why? I think that Elizabeth gave me the car so that I would find the locket and write her story. Was it a love story? I suppose, in a way, it was. I am glad it was not mine.

I could not go through what Elizabeth went through - all those years of waiting for what? Did she think it was enough for her to carry on with life, never feeling his arms around her or hearing the sound of his voice? This is Elizabeth's story. Once again, I am glad it was not my story, as I would never have had the strength to carry on as Elizabeth did. I have since found out that Elizabeth and Bobby are together now. I am glad she is with Bobby.

I was getting quite excited. I had waited for two years, and it was nearly 6:00 o'clock. I kept on looking through the window - waiting. Then I heard my grandfather knocking on the window. "It is here." he kept on calling.

I looked out of the window, and there, coming up the drive, was my first beautiful car. I ran to the door just in time to see my grandfather waving at the driver.

Another moment, he would have backed into the back door, but all we could do was laugh.

It would have been two years since I first saw the car. I missed the bus, so I had to ride my bicycle to work. The traffic had been diverted through the back streets, and I thought to myself that all these years, I had lived here and had never been down the back streets before.

As I stopped to let the traffic go by, I watched an old lady getting out of the car. I think it must have been her nephew who was holding the door open for her. It was the car that I noticed first; it was a very strange green. The old lady must have seen me looking at her, so she waved. As I was smiling back at her, she fell to the floor. I dropped my bicycle and ran towards her. The young man and I picked her up, and he asked if I could help him get her into the house.

He smiled as we both lifted the old lady into the house. He asked if I could drive the car around the back for her, as he was not allowed to drive. I smiled and said I would make her a cup of tea first and then move the car.

When I knew that Elizabeth was ok, I took the keys from the sideboard and told the young man I would move the car and put it into the garage.

I sat in the car for a few minutes. It was the most beautiful thing I had seen. I just sat there feeling the steering wheel and admiring the beautiful upholstery. I hoped that one day I would be lucky enough to have a car just like this one. As I drove the car into the garage, I took one last look and closed the door. I popped my head around the corner and placed the keys back onto the sideboard. No one was there, so I picked up my bicycle and cycled off to work.

I worked in a florist shop called J. J's. My boss was a very nice woman - a widow at about 35 years of age. I apologised immediately and explained why I was late. She said that there was not much to do anyway. A couple of weeks later, I popped in to see Elizabeth the lady with the beautiful car. She said, "I am so glad you came."

She put the kettle on. In the next breath, she asked, "Could I be so bold as to ask that if you have a moment, would you be kind enough to drive me to the post office? You see, my old eyes are not as good as they once were." I could not believe my luck. I said yes straight away, so for the next twelve months, I drove Elizabeth around. I swore from that day on. I would save up and buy a car just like the one Elizabeth had.

Early one morning, six months later, her nephew came around and told me that she had died peacefully and that she was grateful for the time she had spent with me. Then he told me that Elizabeth had left me something in her will. I told him that I did not want anything.

He said, "Then what am I going to do with the car? She told me I must give it to you." I asked, "What about you? Did you not want it?" The young man looked and replied, "No, thank you, it is not my kind of car." He said he had taken the liberty to bring it around tomorrow morning if that was ok. I nearly fainted with excitement.

So here I am with the keys in my hand, sitting in my car with the beautiful upholstery all around me.

Grandfather asked, "Where should we go?" I looked at him as he sat beside me and replied, "Anywhere you would like to go." He said, "To the beach." So off we went. We both had a beautiful day together. I could not believe that the car was mine.

I asked my grandfather to pinch me to make sure I was not dreaming. When we arrived home, I wanted to clean the car properly, but my grandfather said, "It is getting late, so we will both clean the car tomorrow." I reluctantly walked away and said to the car, *I will clean you tomorrow.* Grandfather said, "If you are not careful, the car will answer you back." We both laughed together.

The following morning, I was up at six-thirty with my cleaning bucket and clothes. I thought I would start with the upholstery, which was perfect.

I slid my clothes down the back so as not to miss any of the dust something caught on the cloth. As I gently pulled it, I noticed it was a gold chain. I had a bit of a job to pull the rest out. When it finally came free, I saw a beautiful heart-shaped locket.

There were two people smiling back at me. I think the lady would have been very young - about eighteen- and the boy would not have been much older. I went into the kitchen and showed Grandfather the locket. He said, "You must return it." After we had finished cleaning the car, we drove around to Elizabeth's nephew and told him what we had found. He said, "Please do not take this the wrong way, but I am not interested in the locket. By the way, Elizabeth left this box of photographs and letters for you. I was just going to throw them away. If you would like them, you can have them." I took them rather quickly and held them tightly.

"It is a gold necklace. Are you sure you do not want it?" I asked. He replied, "What would I do with a gold heart and chain? No, thank you. I do not want it." My grandfather and I both looked at each other, turned and walked away.

I carefully placed the box on the back seat and said to Grandfather, "Well, what do you think of that?" He shrugged his shoulders and said he did not know.

We drove on, not saying another word to each other. When we arrived home, Grandfather put the kettle on, and we sat there both looking at the box on the table. Grandfather said, "Are you going to open it?" I said, "Should I? They are not my letters.

Grandfather said that they are not his either. "I am sure that she wanted you to have them. See, she put your name on the front." He said. "Maybe she left them for you to read. Maybe she did not want her life thrown away in the trash can."

I thought for a moment. I picked up one of the letters and started to read. I watched Grandfather as he gently took one out and opened it. It was

Elizabeth's writing saying that she had just met the most handsome man that you could ever imagine. His name was Bobby, and she had been invited to a garden party to celebrate her brother's 21st birthday.

He said that some of his friends were coming today and that they had signed up for the Navy.

I asked what they wanted to do that for. He said that there was a war coming.

He also said that he wanted to go, but I could not pass the medical. I looked and said, "Thank God for that." My heart took a flip - what a handsome man he was. He took my hand and kissed it. I pulled my hand away very quickly as my brother said, "Hey, that is my sister Elizabeth." Bobby said, "My apologies. May I take you to the dance?" "I do not know yet." my brother said. "It depends on how well you behave for the rest of the day." "Yes, sir!" Bobbie saluted with a laugh. I walked away with a friend, turning back once more as he caught my eye and gave me a wink.

The dance came and he was waiting for me. The letter read on - what a wonderful night we both had, we had two more wonderful weeks and we spent every hour we could together. I loved him so, then the news came, and he was gone. I wrote every day, waiting for his letters to come.

He said he was going on leave and I could meet him at the station. My brother drove me there and waited patiently. The train arrived at 3.30 in the afternoon, and my brother left shortly after.

We went into the little cafe across the road. Bobby told me how much he loved me from the first day we met and that he would always love me. He asked me to wait for him that he would return and we would get married.

Three months passed, and the letters were getting shorter; then, I heard that he had been injured and that they were trying to get him home. I was so upset, and then one day a letter arrived. My hands were shaking as I tried to open the letter.

Bobby's letter said that he would arrive in two days by ship. He told me how much he loved me and that we would always be together. I held the letter to my heart and screamed out *he's coming home*.

We were listening to the news that evening, Elizabeth wrote. Many ships were destroyed that week. I prayed that his ship would bring him home safely to me.

The time was getting closer. Elizabeth wrote she was getting excited. She had just finished getting dressed when she heard her brother knocking on the door. She shouted immediately, "I am coming." but her brother was already inside, holding a letter in his hand. Elizabeth knew something was wrong. She took the letter from her brother's hand and sat down.

The letter read: *I am sorry to tell you that all hands on board went down* - nothing more, nothing less. Elizabeth stood up and walked out of the room.

Three years later, Elizabeth was reading a newspaper article about the ship that went down with all hands on board. She did not want to read anymore, but as she tried to put the paper down, something drew her to the list of deaths.

She looked again but could not find Bobby's name. She called her brother, telling him what she had found; her brother said that he would go and make some inquiries.

All Elizabeth could think of *was that Bobby was still alive.* When her brother arrived, he said that he would take her to see the person in charge first thing in the morning.

When the morning arrived, Elizabeth was already waiting. They jumped into a taxi, and twenty minutes later, Elizabeth and her brother were asked to sit down.   A few minutes later, a young lass ushered them into the office, where a straight-faced gentleman stood.

"Please sit down," he said with a loud voice. He went on to explain that Bobby was never really on that ship - that he had been badly injured before he was to board the ship.   Elizabeth quickly asked, "Why wasn't I informed?" The stout gentleman said, "Because you were not the next of kin. Since then, his mother has passed away, and Bobby is on his own and will need someone to look after him." Elizabeth looked shocked. Elizabeth's brother asked where Bobby was now. The stout gentleman said, "In a home for retired officers. That is the only place that we could find to put him.

He does not really belong there as it is only for officers." Elizabeth stood up and said, "I want to go and see him." The stout gentleman asked someone to order a taxi, and we went off. I had to read

Elizabeth's letter over again as I could not believe what I was reading. Then Elizabeth said that when she got there, she was afraid to go into the room. How would he take it seeing her again?

She sat down with her brother and asked. "Am I doing the right thing? I still love him with all my heart. Why did he not want me to see him?" Her brother said, "Well, we should see what he has to say. He has nowhere else to go. They say that they were thinking of putting him in a sanatorium."

Elizabeth stood up, walked to the side of his bed and held his hand. Whispering in his ear, "Bobby, it is Elizabeth." She stared into his eyes, but they were empty. Elizabeth bent down and kissed him gently on the cheek, crying out, "Where are you, Bobby? I love you."

Still, nothing came into his empty eyes. He never moved an inch. He just lay there. Elizabeth's brother organised an ambulance to bring him home. That is the way it was for the next 42 years. Elizabeth spent her time talking to Bobby every day. Holding his hand, she used to say to her brother, "Bobby spoke to me today."

Her brother knew he never did, Elizabeth never married; she was by Bobby's side until his death. It was a strange day when Bobby passed away. Elizabeth said, I had just come in with some daffodils, bent forward and kissed him; I was sitting there as usual and asked him, "What do you think of the flowers, my dear?" As I turned around, I swear I saw Bobby's eyes follow me to the door. I felt him squeeze my hand before he took his last breath.

I called my brother and told him that Bobby had just passed away. Elizabeth sat down and held his hand, talking to him and telling him she would always love him. Her brother arrived, and Elizabeth told him what she had seen. "I told you he loved me."

I slowly put the letters on the table and thought of all the years Elizabeth had spent looking after Billy as I waited for my grandfather to finish reading Elizabeth's letter. I said, "I do not think I could look after someone for forty-two years." My grandfather said, "If you really loved someone, you would."

5.   The End of The Story

When I started to listen to this story, I saw a young girl on her hands and knees scrubbing the floors.

I do not think she minded the job that she was doing, but I knew she was very lonely as I could hear her talking to herself. I picked up her thoughts through her memories. I remember thinking she was lonely and needed a friend.

But is it friendship we crave, or is it answers to our questions?   When we no longer believe in God, we question why there is so much heartache in the world.

You be the judge of that.

It was getting quite cold, so I wrapped my shawl even tighter around me. I remembered the hundred times I had stood here, looking out over the great wall surrounding the convent. It was a lifetime ago since I was dropped off at the front gate as a young girl at the Sisters' house.

I remember thinking, *"How would I ever get out?"* I clenched my bag tightly to myself and felt a push from behind. I remember my mama's last words: *Try to be a good girl.* As she pushed me through the door, I did not look back; there was no need to. I knew that she had left before I had a chance to look around.

Someone pulled on my shirt sleeve and beckoned me to follow, and I did for the rest of my life.

I suppose it was during the first five years that it was very hard work, and everything we did was around the Morning Prayer, which was the start of the day, and the last prayer for the evening was the end of the day — in between, seemed like the same thing, day in and day out.

I had been here for about seven years when someone new came. I say *new,* but she had already been in the convent for four years.

At first, we were not allowed to talk - we talked with our eyes and got quite clever at expressing what we needed to say to each other.

I remember our first meeting when she slipped me a piece of paper asking me to meet her behind the chapel in the small garden. After the prayer meeting, my first instinct was to panic, but then some of my old self crept through, and I asked *why not.*

So here I am, waiting for her. I hear a noise just behind me, then a tap on my shoulder and there she is. Her eyes were very bright, and she had a beautiful smile. I looked around, and the stillness was upsetting. It had been a long time since I had had a personal conversation. We sat together with our arms wrapped around our legs on the floor, just talking.

She said that her parents had put her under the care of the nuns a long time ago. I told her a similar story of how I came to be here, too. Do not get me wrong, it was a place of great knowledge and comfort, but it could also be a place of great loneliness. It is strange, but the first question my newfound friend Alicia asked was, "Why do you believe in God?" What a strange question to be asking, I thought.

She had been in the care of the nuns for the past fourteen years. She asked again, "Do you believe in God?" I said, "Yes, of course I do." She asked again, "Why?" I replied, "Why not?"

Once again, she asked, "Do you really know that He is here?" With that, she said, "Then why did He not hear my cries for help? Why doesn't he hear the cries of others?" She said, "Such as the other day, the plane that crashed and all on board were lost. Where was He then?" I thought for a moment and remembered back a long time ago.

My first introduction to the good Lord was when Mama used to say a prayer asking for different things. She always did the sign of the cross, and then, as she turned away, she would slap me or one of the other children. She would shout so much that she would spit out every hateful word. She constantly told me the devil would take me away and that God was there to judge me.

Why had I not asked the same question before? Why had I just been led by the hand and then introduced to the Lord by prayer or by silence?

I thought of how many times I had said the same prayer over and over again. Did the good Lord hear my prayer? I never left the convent to understand what was going on in the outside world. Now and again, I heard little rumours, but we did not really understand anything outside of these walls.

We both sat very quietly after that, and Alicia said that it was time to go. She gently placed her hand on my arm. It felt good, so I placed my hand on the top of hers and knew that we would always be friends.

I asked if we could meet again tomorrow evening. She said, "Not tomorrow," that it would be too hard. "Could we make it the following evening?" I said, "Yes, of course." Alicia went first, and I followed. The night was quite beautiful - the stars were shining brightly, and the moon was on its side as we quickly walked back through the gate.

The following morning, we just lifted our eyes to each other as if to say good morning. The days after that were different - from somewhere deep inside me, I felt a growing comfort, and I felt alive.

The following night, I lay there trying to answer some of Alicia's questions. I remembered her words about the aeroplane crash and that all aboard were lost. I remember lying back in my bed and asking for help. Someone gently tapped on my foot and said, "The Lord did not make the aeroplane fall from the sky. It was a man-made - man's dilemma, and I am sorry to say that it was a mechanical fault.

I thought about her words, and yes, it made a lot of sense; why do we so readily blame the good Lord for everything that goes wrong? I thought once more about when my mama shuffled me through the gates. I thought of all the times I asked, *why did you do this to me? Did you hate me so much?* I asked the good Lord many times.

Then, someone again touched my thoughts and said, "It is time for you to understand more, but you have to listen to your soul. Your time is now getting close when you must leave the convent and venture out into the world. Your work now lies outside of the convent." I thought I must have been dreaming. I met Alicia the following night and told her what I had heard about the aeroplane. She smiled and said, "That makes a lot of sense." I also told her about someone talking to me, telling me that I would be working outside of the convent. She said, "It would take a miracle to get you outside these walls." We just laughed together, and then I said to her, "It was strange you were asking those questions. When you really come to understand more of the world, 95% of things that happen to us are what we have ourselves brought on."

God did not make the aeroplanes; God does not make children sick. Only bad management of the earth does that.

We have produced so many chemicals in our food and water that we no longer keep track of what is good and what is not good to eat and drink. I thought for a moment, then said to Alicia, "I suppose when you think about it, not many of our companions get sick, and yes, it is true, age is the cause of death here in this convent." She thought for a moment and said, "That's true. In the fourteen years I have been here, I've never really got sick except for women's problems, but that is normal, by the way."

Alicia is her real name. Mary is the name the church gave to her. My name is Pat, but the church gave me the name Teresa. I do not think I can ever live up to being such a wonderful person as Sister Teresa. Once again, it was time to go, just as I closed the gates behind me.

Then, one of the sisters left me at the door of Mother Superior. I thought, *what is going to happen to me now?* The door opened, and I was asked to come in. Mother Superior asked me to sit down and straight away told me that I had been here long enough to know the rules and that it was not the place to remind me. In the next breath, she said that I would be leaving tomorrow morning to work outside the convent, helping the people adjust. I wondered what she meant, but I just knew I could never question her authority. I just bowed my head and walked away.

The following morning at 4:00 am, I was up, showered and shown to the gate. I had already taken off my habit and been given clothes fit for the streets, which were not kind to me in any way - they just fell off me like a sack. I looked at the beautiful sun shining, took a deep breath and knew that I was beginning my new life.

I spent many happy hours with the people from the village. I did not preach to them, and I loved them instead. I told them stories about the Lord - of his happy times on the earth. I did not want to tell them about His suffering. I wanted the people to remember the Lord with love and kindness and happy memories of how Jesus would go out and talk to the people. I told them how He would heal the sick and give water to those who could not drink, but most of all, I told them to respect God and His Son. We always had the memories of the happy times that Jesus had while on this earth.

We all know the suffering that went on, but times have changed, and the memories of Jesus happily walking amongst his people gave them hope once more. Many years have passed now.

I remembered my friend Alicia, and I talked about all those years gone by. I did not have much sickness; I only drank through the water that I drank, so I learned to boil everything. I am sitting here looking at the letter that I hold in my hand, afraid to open it; I must. The letter reads that it is time for me to return to the convent to finish my days there as a teacher from the outside world. I also found a new hope, thinking of all the new girls that I would be teaching.

I remember Alicia with a smile and wonder if she is still there.

Once more, I wrap the shawl around my shoulders as I stand and look out to the great walls that once surrounded me. I am happy to be standing here. I have a roof over my head, a warm bed to lie on, food in my belly and a lifetime of memories. What more could I ask for?

6. The Pillow

I *do not know about forgiveness, as I was brought up in an environment of everlasting relationships.*

My parent's love lasted forever. What you are taught throughout your life, you believe, will hopefully last you for the rest of your life. Can you experience something that you never thought possible - the man you thought loved you and thought that he would love you too, until the end of time?

You keep asking yourself, where did you go wrong? What did you do to make him stop loving me, and when did it start? I have asked these questions time and time again: more importantly, could I trust and love again, and could I forgive? I do not think so.

The Pillow

I awoke once again to find my pillow wet with tears. Every night, I cry myself to sleep. Will I ever get over the hurt and loneliness? I ask myself a million times. Why did this have to happen? No answer ever comes back.

As I slowly rose from the bed and walked to the window, I pulled the curtains back and then closed them quickly. I am not ready for a new day just yet. I walk into the kitchen and put the kettle on. It is half past four in the morning. I remember the phone call, grabbed my coat, forgot to lock the door, and ran into the accident.

Only two blocks away, I see my husband Scott's car. The ambulance is there, and the next moment, I run towards the trolley. The ambulance man quickly pushes the trolley inside the ambulance as a police officer grabs my arm and pulls me away. "I am sorry," the officer said. "He had already gone when we arrived. The other young lady was taken to the hospital. She is in a serious condition. I am sorry that we could not find any identification on her. Would you know what her name is?" I said, "I am sorry," not realising what I was saying, "What young lady?" I asked, pulling on the young policeman's arm. "The young lady who was in the car with your husband." He replied. "I do not know a young lady." I kept on shouting.

The young police officer took me to where another ambulance was waiting. He gently sat me down and explained to the ambulance man that I was in shock. The other man asked me if he could give me an injection to calm me down.

I screamed, "Do you understand, my husband is dead." "Yes, I am so sorry," he replied. "I think you should come along with me to the hospital. I think you need someone to talk to, and it would be a good time to fill in the details while you are there." I let him open the door and put me in the front seat. We slowly drove to the hospital.

When we arrived, the nurse asked, "Are you Mrs Bentham?" I looked and said, "Yes." She asked me if I would follow her to the office. I slowly walked behind her, trying to take in all that had happened. She asked me to take a seat, and I would like a cup of coffee. I said, "Yes" She started to ask me questions about my husband. Thousands of thoughts were going through my mind. I kept asking myself what he was doing on the road at that time of night and who the young lady was.

The nurse then asked me the same question. Do you know the person who was in your husband's car? I looked at her and replied, "No." "I am sorry; she said her name was Lucy." That is all the information she had about the young lady.

The nurse asked if I knew whether she worked with my husband. I said I had never heard of her until today. She asked me if I would go and see if I could recognise her.

I found myself standing up without saying a word and walking behind the nurse. When we arrived, there were machines with leads coming from everywhere, and three doctors were rushing around the young lady. I looked at her, but I did not recognise the person lying there. *Who was she*?

I looked at my watch, and the time read seven-thirty. I apologised and said it was time for me to go. The nurse said she would call a taxi for me. When I arrived home, I put the key into the lock, not realising what I was doing, and then put the kettle on. I looked through the open window but could not see anything - it was pitch black. I heard myself scream, "What is happening?" I found myself on the floor.

I slowly got up and went to bed. I took hold of Scott's pillow and cried myself to sleep.

The Pillow

When I woke up, I started to question myself. Looking back over the last few weeks, Scott and I did not talk much. In fact, we did not do anything together anymore. Why didn't I realise something was happening?

So many things started to take form in my mind: the phone ringing and Scott saying, "It is for me. I will take it in the bedroom." He would come out with a guilty look, but I did not take any notice. Other things seem to preoccupy my mind.

Things seem to become clearer now. All of a sudden, I was looking at things differently. It is easier to look back when you cannot look forward. Still clinging to the pillow, tears come rushing through again the photograph by the side of the bed; my husband's shirt lazily put on the chair, and the coat was thrown on the bedpost. Ho, God. He will never pick up his trousers again or take his coat off the bed. When does it all stop?

The Pillow

I cannot stop the tears from falling on the pillow. The next few days were the hardest I have ever had to live through. The funeral will be in four days. People tell me once the funeral is over, it becomes easier. I wonder.

Three months have passed, and I am more confused than I was before. The days seem longer. I did love him; if only I had the chance to tell him again. Nobody knocks on the door, nobody phones. I think people are afraid to look me in the face.

As I lie back down on the bed and lay my head on Scott's pillow, my mind goes racing back to the young lady who was in the car crash with him. I started to wonder about her and wanted to know more about this young lady.

Was she my husband's lover? Tomorrow, I will find out. When I arrived at the hospital, she had already been discharged. A nice nurse gave me the address, thinking that I was her next of kin.

I find myself sitting outside her house, wondering if Scott ever came here. I find myself walking up the steps and ringing the bell. A young voice answered, saying, "The door is open; please come in." The door automatically closes behind me as I start to climb up the stairs.

Before I could knock, the door opened, and the young lady said, "Would you like to come in?" The next moment, I could hear myself shouting and screaming, telling her how much I hated her, telling her that she would burn in hell. I watched her slowly fall to the floor. I walked away and left her there. I never went back.

The pain would not go away. Then, one morning, I found myself tying the rope to the roof, standing on a chair, looking up at all the beautiful timber that Scott and I chose when we built this house together.

The Pillow

That was my last look at life as I slowly kicked the chair from underneath me. The pain, at last, was gone. It is strange when you do get to the other side. It is the pain that you cause another person, and that is the heartache, not the pain other people give to you.

I don't feel that I am where I am supposed to be for some reason or other. I feel a calling. I tried to remember many things, but the only thing that seemed to be prominent was the young lady's memory and the harsh words I said to her. Those words seem to be weighing heavier and heavier on my soul.

I feel that it is the time I tried to make things right. I am not quite sure how I will go about this, but I am sure that this is what I am supposed to do.

As quickly as my mind can comprehend, I find myself standing in a familiar room. I look across, and there is a person I do not recognise.

The Pillow

She is old and frail, and her eyes are closed. As I walk towards the bed, I can feel her calling me. I see the lady's features change back into that beautiful young lady that I remember so well.

Then, just as quickly, she is back as she was when I first saw her - old and frail. She is holding her hand out to me; her eyes are begging me to come forward. I walk towards her and sit on the bed. Her eyes shoot open, and she asks, "Can you ever forgive me?" I took her into my arms, and gently kissed her forehead and whispered, "Yes." And at that moment, I felt my soul getting lighter.

She looked at me with huge, sad eyes. I look back with all the compassion that I held in my memory. The next moment, we are walking across the other side, and we are laughing together, as good friends should.

7.   Was It Just A Moment Ago?

Was it just a moment ago? It feels like forever. Where am I? Am I sitting in the park? I do not know how long I have been here. Something feels familiar, but I fear my senses are stronger than my eyesight.

I pinch myself on my arm; yes, I can still feel the pinch. I know something has changed, but I do not understand why. I feel as though I am talking, but there is no sound coming out of my mouth. I start to panic as everything seems to be locked inside.

I hear someone calling my name. I think it's my name - it sounds familiar, "David!" the person calls again. As quickly as the fear comes over me, peace and tranquillity follow. I feel comforted once more. I am too afraid to leave or to think.

I close my eyes and try to shut myself off from what and why I don't know. Strange flashes of memories come flooding into the car.

I watch my things sliding away from me to the other side of the dashboard. All of a sudden, the car starts to descend the hill. My mind goes racing back *-who will miss me? Did I leave someone behind? Can this really be happening to me? Is this some kind of dream?* I look at the person next to me in the car, but Lizzie is not moving. I close my eyes, but I can hear Peter screaming in the back of the car. I try to shut it out, but it is too loud. I open my eyes, and everything seems to be in slow motion. The car is going down into the water. We are being tossed about. I tried to reach out to my friend Lizzie, but I could not. My heart is racing.

I cannot think, but everything seems to have slowed down to a stop. I thought, if only I could turn back the clock. I thought of all the people who once loved me. I was some brat. I grew up thinking that I always had to prove something.

Nice people did not want to be friends with me anymore. I found myself mixing with what my aunties calls the lower class, the drudges of the earth. I remember thinking to myself that they do not know anything. Turning around and walking away, I always thought I would get back at them somewhere.

Back in the car, I heard myself screaming. I felt my body being pushed further toward Lizzie. My God, her eyes are still open. I know that she is dead. I hear a huge whoosh noise.

I watch the car as it slowly goes deeper into the water. I have to get out of here. I grab the window to pull it down, but it is stuck. I push the door to open, but nothing happens as the water floods in. I loosen the seatbelt to find myself in the back of the car. I know if I could just move one of the bodies, I may be able to wind the window down.

I pull but cannot move my body from the window. I am frantic as the car is filling up with water. I can see bubbles coming out of my mouth. I slowly call for someone to help me get out. There is no one here. My screams go on. I feel myself fall back, but there are no more gasps of air left in me.

No more fighting; the air was being replaced by water. I feel myself lying back with the other two friends. I know my mind is still working. I heard the car bump when it hit the water.

I hear the air coming from one of the two people in the back as the air is pushed out of their throat. I do not believe in God, but I wish he were here with me now. I remember shouting, "God, please help me!" I find myself back in the park, but the question is, "What am I doing here?" It has started to get cold. The snow is just starting to fall.

Was It Just A Moment Ago?

I know I have memories of the snow, but I cannot remember them. I slowly walk over to one of the swings and find myself sitting there.

Then I hear children laughing. I look across, and there are two people sitting on a bench. I look again and think one of them looks familiar. Familiar with what, I do not remember. I find myself sitting there swinging every day, and it seems to go on forever. I don't know why I am here; I just know I have to sit here and wait.

Then, one day, as I am swinging, one of the older ladies falls to the ground. Her friend rushes over to her. She grabs her hand and tells her everything is going to be fine. I immediately feel myself walking over to where she is lying, and I stand by her side. Someone had called an ambulance, and I heard the sirens coming towards us. One of the men got out of the ambulance, bent down to check her pulse at the side of her neck, and said, "I am sorry, she has gone."

I look down and see that she is looking up at me. She calls out to me, "Please do not let them take me away. I am scared." "Scared of what?" I ask. She said, "I do not know. I don't want to die yet." I ask, "Are you dead?" She looked at me, saying, "I think so." I look back and say, "Then why are you afraid of dying?" She started to stand up and grabbed hold of my hand. She looks back to the floor and sees herself lying there. She panics; I place my arms around her shoulder, telling her everything is going to be okay. I slowly walk away from the incident and take her to another park bench. She asks, "What are they going to do with me?" "Does it really matter?" I ask. She looked at me without saying a word. We just sat there together. I asked her what her name was. She said "Maureen," but everyone who knew her used to call her Mona. I asked, "Why?" She replied that she had the nickname since she was 12 years old. I thought for a moment, and I started to remember something. I shook my head, trying to remember. It was that name *Mona*. We sat there for quite a long time, not saying a word.

Then we heard the children laughing. I asked her if she had any children. She said, "No." but she told me that she had a sister who died very young and she had a young child. She was left to bring the child up but was afraid of children having none of her own. She said it was difficult. He was quite a smart little fellow, but she could not control him in the end. She looked at me with huge, sad eyes and said, "I did love him. I tried many times to tell him, but he always walked away."

I felt very sad for this woman. I asked, "Did the boy love you?" She said, "I will never know now."

She looked down at her feet and said he died 35 years ago. I gently placed my arm around her shoulder and told her I was very sorry to hear that. She looked up at me and said, "You remind me of him." She said, "It is the eyes, you know. You never forget their eyes."

My David had the most beautiful blue eyes you had ever seen. My heart started pounding in my chest; the memories came flooding back. "What happened to David?" I asked. She said, "David died in a car crash. The car went off the road into the water. They found their bodies three days later. I will never forget the look on his face when they brought him up."

I held her tighter and felt myself kissing her on the forehead and telling her, "I am sure David loved you very much but did not know how to say it." She looked into my eyes and said, "Do you think so?"

I looked into her eyes, holding her even tighter, telling her, "Yes, I know David loves you very much." I felt the warmth come into my body. There was a bright light right in front of me. I heard someone say, "Well done, David, well done." I felt

Mona's hand grasping mine very tightly. She said, "Would you come with me? I am afraid to go on my own." I squeezed her hand and said, "Let's go together." She giggled and looked up at me with so much love. I looked back, knowing that this is why I was sent back - this was my penance.

8. Today, Or Was It Yesterday?

Today, or was it yesterday or maybe last week? Well, it could have been a month ago, but I cannot remember. I cannot seem to remember what happened today. I used to have such a good memory. I lean back in my chair, feeling my eyes closing. I take a deep breath and think, *if only I could remember.*

I find my thoughts going back to when I was seven years old. I can see the cobblestones. I can hear people laughing in the background. I can see Mother hanging out the washing.

Just then, my friend called me, and my memories awakened. We would walk down the back lane to our special spot. It was a place that people called Lover's Lane. To us, it was a place where we could dream together.

Today, Or Was It Yesterday?

My friend Jean and I would lie on the grass, side by side, talking and laughing about what we would do in the future. I remember saying, "One day, I will be a great lady." She laughed and said, "You would have to talk better than what you do now to be a great lady."

She was the only one who really understood me. In fact, who could understand the words that came out through the stuttering? I could not get many words out. People always came and finished off my sentences, so I got to the point where I stopped talking to people, but my friend Jean seemed to understand every word I could not get out.

She never finished my sentences. She always said, "I am listening, go on." That would give me the courage to carry on. I told her that I would like to be a singer. She replied, "I think you can sing well." We both laughed together. It was time to start walking back home as Mom would be mad if I did not get home in time for tea at five o'clock on the dot.

Later, I helped mom do the dishes. I knew seven o'clock was my bedtime, so I had to bathe and prepare for bed. I lay on my bed, thinking, *why do I stammer? None of my friends do, so why me?* I looked out of the window. I love to look at the stars shining. I tried to count them, but I lost count. The lights go out in the street, and I find myself drifting off to sleep.

I heard someone knocking at the door. My eyes shoot open as I find myself back in the easy chair. Calling out, "I will be there in a moment," Jean stood there and said, "Why did you lock the door? I told you not to lock the door." I just looked at her and thought she was always bad-tempered. I asked, "Would you like a cup of tea?" She replied, "No, I am going to the shops.

Today, Or Was It Yesterday?

Do you want me to bring you anything back?" I looked around and said, "No thanks." She looked at me, asking, "Did you make a list?" I said, "What list?" She gave me that look and said, "The shopping list. I told you to write down what you needed."

She walked to the kitchen sink, saying, "You never write anything down." She opened the fridge and said, "You need milk. What are you going to have for tea?" I just looked at her. I just stood there, not saying a word. She took my purse out of the drawer and took out some coins. "Is this all you've got?" I said, "I have not been to the post office yet." She said, "What am I going to do with you?" I just smiled.

She said, "Give me your pension book." I took it out of the drawer and signed it. It seemed like a long time before Jean got back with a huge bag of groceries. I asked, "Why did you buy all that food?"

She replied, "Because if it is there, you might eat it." I smiled and thought, what a good friend she is. The next moment, she was gone. I looked around and wondered what I was going to cook for tea.

The next moment, the doorbell rang. A young man stood there asking me if I wanted my windows cleaned. I asked him, "Are they dirty?" He replied, "Yes." I asked him how much it would cost me. He replied, "A cup of tea." I smiled at him and said, "Okay." Not long after, he was knocking on the door again. I told him to come in and sit down as I was just putting the kettle on. He asked if I lived here alone. I said, "Yes." I turned around to get the cups down, and something hit my head. I tried to call out, but I could not get anything out. I heard Jean's words over and over again, "Do not open the door to anyone." Then everything went black.

I heard sirens in the background. I heard my friend Jean calling me. I tried to tell her I was sorry for not listening to her. I felt the stammer coming back and could not get my words out. I felt the pounding in my head, then remembered the young man. What a silly old fool I am.

Once again, my mind slips back to when I was seven years old. I found myself sitting on the cobblestones once more, but this time, it was different - nothing seemed to move. It did not seem to me as if I was sitting there looking around; everything felt strange, but I recognised my street. *What is happening to me*?

I looked up at the sky, and it felt different. I don't seem to sense anything or feel anything. My mind seems to be wandering a lot more now, and I seem to be remembering things that I couldn't remember from yesterday. I heard a strange voice saying, "Let her go, let her go." I swear that was Jean's voice.

What does she mean, *let her go*? I find myself still not able to move; looking down at my hands, things seem to be changing; my body is getting younger. I felt the strength coming into my body, and then, for some unknown reason, I started to stand up, and as I did, the street started to change.

I hear music coming from one of the houses, and my grandmother calls me. I was thinking, *how can I hear my grandmother when she's dead? B*ut I didn't question it anymore. I just started to walk towards Grandma's house.

The cat was the first thing to greet me- I love my grandma's cat. Grandmother just said, "Close the door, love, it is starting to get chilly". She beckoned me to sit down in the chair. I never seemed to question anything; I just felt so at home here, as if nothing had changed.

Then my grandmother asked if I wanted to stay. I thought that was a silly question to ask me. I just looked at her, and she told me to look out the window. I did not question why I just did it. I did not recognise anything because everything had changed. My house had gone. Where was Jean?

I was back on my old street, but the house was different - somebody had painted my house, someone had taken the old gate off, and someone had put a new one on. *What is going on?* I cannot seem to figure things out. I ask my friend Jean, "Where the bloody hell are you?" I look around and see someone sitting in the old seat in the park. I walk across to her, asking, "Do you know where Jean is"

"The woman puts her hand on the seat next to her and gently taps it, saying, "Sit down love." I sat down beside her. I could not take it all in.

The woman asked me, "What do you remember?" I thought for a moment and replied, "I don't know." *What is she talking about?* I looked at her and asked, "Please find my Jean for me, as we have been friends all our lives, and I miss her so much".

The woman said, "You have to understand what happened to you before you can find your friend Jean. The woman gently put her arm around my shoulder and pulled me towards her, asking, "Can you remember the last thing that happened?" I tried very hard, and then I remembered the young man and a cup of tea.

She asked, "Did you remember the hospital?" "No," I said and then things started to happen.

I closed my eyes, and I could feel my head hurting. I could feel someone lifting me up, and I could hear the ambulance siren. Everything started to get hazy. I heard people shouting, and in the midst of everything that was happening, I heard my Jean tell me, "Everything is going to be okay love".

I remember thinking, I can close my eyes now; my Jean is here. Then, once again, I heard the woman who was sitting beside me asking, "Are you ready now?" It felt like I had been wandering for years, looking for my Jeanie. I was feeling pretty tired. I closed my eyes and heard Jean calling me, "I'm coming." I replied, "I'm coming too.

9. The Piano Lessons

I was sitting at my desk, daydreaming, when I felt a young girl standing behind me saying, "You have to believe that things are meant to happen and dreams do come true. You just have to believe in yourself."

She sat down beside me and said, "You never know when and where, but someone sends you help when you least expect it. I looked at her and said, "Yes, they do." We both smiled together and just sat there.

I shook with excitement as I had waited all my life for this moment, and here it was. Mother came to straighten my dress and tidy my hair as we waited to be called onto the stage.

Was this really happening? I could not believe it. It seemed like such a long time ago, and the memories of the piano lessons came rushing back. Things were hard then for Mum and me. Dad, I suppose you can say, came and went. We never saw him again.

Mother tried very hard to bring me up as she had to leave her family behind because, in those days, it was really bad to have an illegitimate daughter. Illegitimate - how I hated that word.

People in the street would whisper behind our backs, and the kids at school would tease me - always calling me *the bastard child,* but Mum was quite determined that I would have as much as she could give me. When I was seven, Mum lost her job, so with everything that was happening, we decided to leave and make a new start.

We moved about 200 kilometres from where we last lived. To us, it was the end of the world. We had been in our new house for about three weeks. I started school the following week and met a new friend named Trish.

Mum managed to get a job at the bakery, and things seemed to be going pretty well for us. People seemed very friendly.

Mother said she had spoken to the man who looks after the building and promised to find someone to come and fix the heater for us as winter was just around the corner.

When Tom knocked at the door, I had to look up to him as he was so tall. He smiled as he put his hand out and introduced himself. I felt all grown up and shook his hand. He said, "Your Mother asked me to fix the heater, and this is the only day I get off, so I thought I would fix it today if that is okay with you." I had never been spoken to like that before, and it made me feel very grown-up. I asked him to come in, and I noticed his long fingers while he was working. I asked, "What kind of work do you do?" He said he was the piano teacher. "Wow!" I said, "I would love to learn how to play." Tom said, "Why not ask your mother, "I said, "Do you really think I could learn to play?" Tom said, "Let us see, okay?" "Yes," I replied, I will ask mum."

Tom left, and when Mother came home, I thought about what he had said. I waited until we were eating tea and asked, "Could I learn to play the piano?" She said, "What gave you that idea?" I said, "Tom." "Who is Tom?" I said, "That man who fixed the radiator - the man who lives upstairs." She said, "I think it would be very expensive, but we will see."

When I got home from school the following day, Tom was there by the door. I said, "I asked mother about the lessons, but she said we could not afford it just yet." Tom replied, "Maybe we could keep it a secret until things get better. What do you think?" I answered back, "Yes, I think that will be fine."

After school every night, I would quickly do my chores and skip up the steps to see Tom. I really did like Tom. He had been teaching me for three months when his mother asked, "What do you do when I am not here?"

I thought for a moment because I didn't want to tell Mother just yet. I said, "Study." She never asked any more questions and said I was a good girl, and that was that. Tom and I continued studying together, and then one day, he said, "You will be the greatest pianist the world has ever seen." I said, "Do you think so?" He replied, "Yes." Tom was not into a lot of conversation, but I remember asking him, "Where is your mother, Tom? Are you married?" I was secretly in love with Tom. He replied, "We must carry on now." "How long have you lived here?" He replied again, saying, "We are here to study," and we did.

Then, one day, a letter came addressed to me, and my mother said, "Who is writing to you?" I said I did not know. She read out the name, To Miss Mandy Cartwright. She handed me the letter and said, "This is your letter, Mandy." This was the first letter that I had ever received in my life.

I opened it very carefully and read *Dear Miss Cartwright. There is a request for you to attend an interview on the 22 of November.* I could not believe what I was reading. Mother said, "What is it, Mandy?" I did not know what to say. She took the letter from my hand and asked, "What interview?" I said, "The music interview." "What music interview?" Mother asked. I said, "The piano music is one that Tom has been teaching me." Mother sat down and said, "How long has he been teaching you?" I said, "Just over two years." Mother went very quiet and said, "I need a cup of tea." She asked me to sit at the table, so we both sat there, and Mother said, "Tell me more about Tom." I told her about the day when I first met Tom. I said, "Do you remember that man who fixed the radiator?" She thought for a moment and said, "I never did get a bill from that man." I said, "Do not worry, Mother."

She picked up the letter, asking me to walk with her. We walked upstairs, and Mother knocked on the door, but nobody answered. She knocked again when the cleaning lady shouted up, "What are you doing up there?" Mother looked over the bannister and shouted down, "I want to speak to Tom." The cleaning woman said, "There is no Tom living there to my knowledge, and there has never been one living there."

My mother said, "Are you sure?" She shouted back, "As sure as I am standing here." My mother looked at me and said, "What has been going on?" I looked at her and said, "I did go in that room, and Tom was always waiting for me." Mother said, "Where is the piano?" I replied, "In that room." She looked at me again and said, "Wait here."

She went downstairs to see the old man who looked after the rooms and asked, "Who lives in the top room?" He looked and said, "No one lives there anymore." She replied, "My daughter told me Tom gives her piano lessons."

He stood up quickly and asked, "What piano lessons?" My mother replied, "For the past two years, he's been teaching her." He said, "That is not possible. Tom has been dead for the last 40 years.

You had better sit down." He said, pulling out a photo of a young man and asking, "Is this the person you are talking about?" My mother said, "I do not know. It was my daughter who had spent the time with him."

She stood up and called, "Come here, Mandy. Come here at once." I immediately started to walk down the stairs. I looked back up for a brief moment, and I swear I could see Tom standing there waiting for me.

My mother asked me to come in and sit down. The old man Ted asked, "Where did you get these crazy stories? You do not know Tom; you never did." At that moment, I looked at the desk and saw Tom's photo. I immediately picked it up and said, "This is Tom.

This man has been teaching me the piano." He looked at my mother and me, sat down with a thud and said, "Tom is my son, and he died 40 years ago.

I shouted back, "No, you are telling me lies. Tom is my best friend and taught me to play the piano."

Mother jumped straight in and asked, "When did you first meet Tom?" I told her that was the day he came to fix the boiler. Ted said, "The room has been closed since my son passed away." Then I told Ted that the piano was over by that window, and we used to look out of the window together."

I also told Ted about the bed in the corner of the room and the photographs of his father and his mother. I also said, "Tom told me that was his father, but that does not look a bit like you." Ted said the photograph was of his mother and him when they were younger, and at that point, Ted broke down and cried. He took one of the keys from the rack, left the room and went upstairs. I followed him as he put the key in the lock and opened the door.

We went in together. The room now was musty, and the curtains were ragged. The bed just seemed such an old bed now, and the piano was covered in dust and not as I remembered it. I told Ted about it, and he started to cry. He said, "I just do not know what is happening." The next moment, I heard Tom's voice. I looked by the door, and he was staring at me. Then he told me he wanted to give me the chance he never had and make him proud of me. He said to tell his father that he loved him very much and that his mother said that everything was going to be okay.

I turned around and told Ted what Tom had told me. Ted could not believe what I was saying until Tom spoke again. He said, "Tell Dad that the music books are under the bed in his bedroom in the tin box." Ted said, "My God!" I looked around again for Tom, but he was not there.

I used to go upstairs and knock on the door, hoping that Tom would open the door to me again and that we could play the piano as we used to. But tonight is my night; I'm back in the concert hall, and I know I will make Tom proud of me. When the instructor calls out my name, I know Tom will be right behind me, cheering me on.

10. The Button Box

Is *it the memories that hold the promise of life itself, or can we hope that we will find the love that we once knew? Are the dreams we had a sign that someone is trying to help us somewhere? Oh God, I hope so.*

Someone gently reached out and held onto my hand as I held out my hand. Once more, I am back in the baker's shop with all my beautiful memories from long ago.

I remember sitting there with the box in my hand, trying to wipe the dust off the lid. Slowly and gently, I opened the lid, and there were the buttons just as I remembered them. I stuck my finger into the centre and gently moved them around. My eyes fall onto the large pink button, and the memories come flooding back.

The Story

Mama's new cardigan was the first Christmas I ever remember, and every one of us received a Christmas present. We were all so excited when Papa handed out the presents on Christmas morning. We watched it with excitement. First, my brother David tore the paper off his present. We all clapped as we watched my sister Jenny gently remove the paper from her present.

Jenny was such a gentle soul, but when she was born, she was quite sick. We did not think she would last the year, but Jenny is seven now, and her smile tells you everything. With a scream of delight, Jenny takes out a rag doll. She holds it very tightly and kisses it. We all laugh as we watch her smile.

She gives mummy the wrapping paper very carefully. Once more, the attention is on the Christmas tree. It is now my turn as Daddy hands me the present and tells me that I have been a good girl and that I deserve the present.

I watch as everyone starts to clap. I feel so excited. It is such a huge present. As I slowly unwrap the present, my mind goes rushing back. I had just walked Jenny to school because the weather was getting colder. As I wrapped my coat further around me, I felt someone tap me on the shoulder. It was old Ben from the baker's shop. "Good morning," he said. I looked up and said, "Good morning." Ben asked me if I had a moment to spare - that he would like to talk to me. Out of the cold, we went into the shop, and he asked me to sit by the fire. I looked around, and the smell was beautiful. It was so warm here, and I wished I could stay here forever. Ben said, "I'm looking for someone to help me in the baker's shop." I spun around and asked, "Are you giving me a job?"

Ben replied, "Yes, but it is not much money." I felt a smile coming across my face. "I will take it," I shouted. Ben smiled and said, "Can you come tomorrow at 3 am?" I stood up and said, "I will be here." I ran all the way home to tell Mother. Mother had not been very well lately. She seemed to be getting sicker each day. She coughs a lot, but Daddy says everything will be okay.

I burst through the door, took off my hat, walked into the kitchen and said to Mother, "I got a job." She looked at me and asked, "Where?" I said, "The baker's shop." Mother sat down and asked, "When?" I replied, "Tomorrow at 3 am." She stood up, put her arms around me, and told me she loved me and how proud she was. I was 11 years old, but everybody said that I had an old head on young shoulders. I don't know what they meant by that, but it made me feel grown-up.

She said she would walk Jenny to school tomorrow morning as she thought I would be too tired. I told Mother that I would finish my job at seven o'clock and came straight home to Jenny. Mother started to cough again. I told her to sit down and that I would make her a nice cup of tea.

I looked at my mother and saw the sadness in her eyes. She looked at me and said, "I am so sorry you grew up so fast. I should be the one working in the baker's shop, not you." I told Mother not to worry that the baker's shop had a lovely smell and was nice and warm.

Mother smiled. Old Ben gave me one and sixpence per week. It was such a lot of money for me. I took the money home every week to Mother, but she would give me the sixpence back. I had saved my sixpence every week for Christmas, which was getting close. Now, I wanted my family to have the best Christmas that they had ever had. Every week, I would look through the shop windows to see what was there. Then, one day, the lady in the shop was putting a rag doll in the window. I knew that would be the perfect present for Jenny. I walked straight into the shop like a grown-up person and said to the lady, "I would like to buy that rag doll for my sister, please."

The nice lady asked me if I would like it wrapped. I said, "Yes, please." So, she took the doll from the window and wrapped it up for me.

It looks so pretty in pink and blue wrapping paper, and she even put a bow in the corner of the present.

I did not want to hold it too tight, as I did not want to squash the paper or the little bow on the corner. I ran all the way home, up the steps, placed the present on top of the wardrobe and gently placed the newspaper on the top so that no one could see it.

Mama asked if I'd had a good day. I said, "A very good day indeed, Mother." For the next few weeks, I looked in the shop window, and sometimes I walked into the shop. The ladies would look at me and ask, "Can I be of some assistance?" I replied most politely, "No, thank you, not at the moment."

Then, one day, as I was looking around the shop, I noticed this beautiful pink cardigan. I knew straight away that I would buy the cardigan for my mother.

Once again, the lady asked, "Would you like me to wrap it?" I said, "Yes, please, but could you wrap it in a different type of paper because this is a present for my mother." The lady replied, "I would be very proud to."

She soon returned with the present, beautifully wrapped. She looked at me, smiled and said, "I hope your mother likes the present." I looked back and said, "I am sure she will." I ran all the way home.

Once again, I put the present on top of the wardrobe. I sat on my bed for a moment and thought, *Mother will love this present. I do not ever remember her having anything new.*

Once again, my mind went back to the Christmas tree as I was opening my present. I had a new pair of pyjamas. I held them up so everyone could see and told Mother, "I will never be cold again." Everyone laughed as I stood up and walked towards the Christmas tree. I wanted to give my mother her present myself.

I bent down, picked it up and handed it to her. Her hands were shaking with excitement as she gently started to open the present. Trying not to tear the paper, Mother looked at me and said, "What the heck!" as she ripped the paper off quickly. Her eyes glowed with excitement.

A little scream of excitement came out of her mouth as she held the pink cardigan up, and tears started to run down her cheeks. She stood up, held out her arms, and said it was the best Christmas she could ever remember.

That night, the house caught fire. I remember sitting on the bed with a box of buttons. When the fire died down, I looked around and found what was left of Mother's new pink cardigan - just one button. Once again, I was looking at the tin box with the buttons.

I looked around, and everything was gone - just chalk remained of what once used to be our home. I could not feel anything. I did not want to move, so I just sat there in case Mother came looking for me. Then, somehow, I was back in the baker's shop and could smell the bread being baked.

As I looked around, I could see a shadow standing there. I could hear her asking, "Are you ready?" I stood up and started to walk towards her, and with every step I took, I could hear Mother calling me.

Then I heard my sister calling. As I held out my hand to the lady who was now standing really close to me, I reached for her hand, and the next moment, it was my mother holding my hand. I could hear the laughter and the love calling me.

As I turned around and looked at the lady, I slowly let go of her hand. I knew she came to help me as I once again felt my mother's arms around me.

11.   Lora Baxton

 This is one story I did not want to listen to at all, as it is too cruel. To think of a young girl going through what she went through, it took me a long time to write this story and the sadness that came with it.

I was there with this young girl as she gently took me through her time on earth. It was not a journey,'' that I wanted to go on. She did not realise that it was about letting go of your memories and the hurt you felt through those memories.

Once you accept the fact that your body is no longer and death has occurred, beautiful things happen all at once. Lora was too afraid. As time went by and somebody disturbed where her body finally rested, she began to realise that she did not have to stay there, and for that one split second, the thought sent out a wavelength to people like myself who waited. It depends on how quickly we can pick it up or hold onto it.

It is still their decision, even then, whether they want to let go of their memories or once again pull back.

I am sorry to say that I lived every moment with what she did. What happened to her? You cannot choose which person comes first; they actually choose you, and once you have made that link, you can never let go. You must go through with them to the end.

Once again, I have lived through someone else's sorrow and pain, and I hope that I will never go through that experience again.

I can see her so plainly - she has dark hair just past her shoulders and a huge blue bow in her hair.

She wears a long-sleeved blouse with a very high neck. Over her blouse is a dark bolero. Her skirt is long, with huge red and black squares. Her socks are like tights, very thick, and worn with black shoes. She wears black-framed glasses with very thick lenses.

I watch her as her mother sends her off to school. There does not appear to be anything wrong, but I watch the child waving to her mother and her mother waving back. I remember the door slamming shut.

My mind is drawn back, as it has been for the last two days, to the floorboards, which are broken and rotted. Some of them are sticking up and are sharp. I know what's under there, but I'm too scared to look. She catches my mind again. Lora will no longer let me stand back as she brings me into her memories.

I am in a kitchen sitting on a huge square sink, where there is a long wooden running board with one tap that comes into the sink. I watch as it drips.

My mother comes into view, and I'm scared. She tells me to drink more water, but I've already drunk three large jugs. I try to cross my legs so that I will not pee my knickers again.

Mother shouts at the top of her voice, "Drink!" and slaps her thigh with a stick. I know I must drink the jug of water now. Before I have finished half the jug, I pee my knickers again.

Mama is going to be so cross with me again as she watches the pee running into the sink and calls me a dirty little girl. Then I was dragged off the sink, and a pillowcase was tied around my wrists as she hung me up on a hook that we used to hang the meat on.

My arms are getting very tired as I ask, "Please, mummy, can I come down now?" I hear her outside the kitchen door, humming a song that she sings in church.

She comes back inside again, pulls off my knickers and throws them in the sink. She keeps hitting me with the stick, calling me a dirty little girl.

She lets me down off the hook and makes me wash my knickers in the sink. I am sitting back on the running board, and I know I will have to wait until she lifts me down.

My eyes are closing, and all I can hear is the drip of that tap. I hate that noise. I opened my eyes as Mother dragged me down and shoved me into a bath of hot water. It is too hot, so I call her, but she only pushes me in deeper.

I know it will not be long now, and she will give me something to eat, put me to bed and read me a story. I will be okay until the morning.

Once more, I am at the door, and I hear that familiar sound as the door bangs shut. I enjoy school, and we have a new teacher named Paula. She is so pretty, and I sometimes think that she likes me the best.

One day, Paula asked, "Why do you always wear long sleeves in the summertime? Why don't you wear something cooler?" I told her that I was not allowed. She smiled at me and said, "Okay."

When I got home, I found myself once again on the running board, but this time, my mind went back to my teacher. My mother wanted to know what I was smiling about. I told her I was thinking about my new teacher, and before I got her name out, the stick came across my legs again, and it hurt so much that I fell off the running board.

Mother was kind to me that night, but before I went to school, she said she would beat me if I said anything to the teacher. I promised her that I would not say anything to the teacher.

While I was having my lunch, the teacher turned my hand over and asked how I got all those bruises. I told her I fell down the steps. She just looked away.

When I got home, my mother asked if the teachers said anything to me. I lied and replied, "No, nothing." The same thing as yesterday happened again. I was on the wooden running board and had to drink three large jugs of water until I peed myself again. I was looking forward to school the following day.

As I was leaving, a stranger knocked on the door and said that he was from the school board.

Mother waved me goodbye as usual, and I turned around and saw the look she had given me.

I was afraid all day long. I wondered what the man had come to see mother about. The teacher kept asking me if I was okay. I said, "Yes, thank you."

It was time to go home, but I was so scared. When I arrived home and opened the door, Mother gave me a big smile. I thought *I was glad everything was okay*.

Before I knew what was happening, she dragged me off my feet, and we were looking into each other's faces. She asked me what I had said at school. I told her, "Nothing." She said, "You must have said something." I said I'd not said anything, but the teacher noticed my bruises, and that is when her hand came across my head so hard that I heard a crack and never felt anything anymore.

The next thing I felt was mommy pulling up the floorboards and placing me at the bottom. She placed four large jugs of water around me, put on my best clothes, and tidied my skirt and blouse so it looked perfect.

She then placed the floorboards back on top of me and walked away. I did not move. I do not know why. I was not afraid; I just lay there waiting - for what I did not know. I was aware of the people who came and went out of the house.

One day, I heard children playing when I heard a voice saying that the bulldozers would come in and knock down the old place. I did not know what a bulldozer was.

I then heard a huge rumbling noise, and the whole house shook. I heard someone saying that he thought he saw a boy in there when everything stopped. I heard people running up and down the stairs into the room, and then I heard the floorboards breaking up and heard someone say there was a body here.

When they took up the rest of the floorboards, the light hurt my eyes. I heard them say, "I think she had been dead for thirty-odd years." I was placed on a stretcher bed. I was scared, wondering where they were taking me. They placed me on the table with a white cloth, and I tried to tell them I was okay, but no one seemed to listen.

Then the lights went out, and I heard someone else in the room asking, "Why are you still here?" I said, "Where was I supposed to go? "Then another person came along and said, "I know you. You used to live in the grand old stone house.

The old girl told everyone that she and her daughter were leaving town to go and visit her parents. We all thought that they'd gone together, but she never came back." Things were making sense now. When I look back, I wonder why I stayed in there so long.

Why did Mother leave me? I listened for a while, trying to understand what they were saying. The older person of the two said, "Well, now, what are you going to do?" I sat up and said, "I don't know." He said, "Then you will never know.

Do you want to stay here all the time?" I said, "No, I don't think so." He said, "You had better make up your mind." I thought of the teacher, and I felt different inside. He smiled at me and said,

"Do you need help to cross over?" He said, "Keep thinking of your teacher. Can you remember her smile?" I nodded and said, "Yes." Just then, I felt someone taking hold of my hand and asking me, "Are you ready to go?" Her hand was warm. I knew she was here to help me. I kept thinking of my teacher.

Something strange was happening - a huge white light was coming closer and closer. Someone was standing there waving to me. I knew who she was; she walked straight towards me and took me in her arms.

I looked up and thought I would recognise that smile anywhere. She smiled at me, and as I let go of the other person's hand, all the pain went with it as we walked away together.

12. The Last Breath

I had just finished gardening, and the sun shone on my beautiful front lawn.

I sat myself down and laid back and stretched my arms out, thinking, what a beautiful day. I thought nothing could take this feeling away. I closed my eyes, and I could smell the flowers.

Then I felt someone lying beside me. I turned around and looked. The next moment, I could feel her take hold of my hand. She just looked at me and said, "Shall we go?" I closed my eyes again, feeling her holding my hand and taking me with her to God knows where.

I listened to her telling me about her journey and meeting with a really nice old gentleman.

When you think that no one in the world cares, someone comes into your life right at the last moment. Somehow, you remember the feeling of kindness.

The old gentleman showed me kindness I would never forget. I hope that when I get to the other side, he is there waiting for me. If he isn't, then I'm going to look for him and give him the biggest hug that anyone could ever give. This is her story.

Waiting for the last breath, I am lying down, looking up at the sky, waiting. I am not going to feel sorry for myself because, for the first time, I cannot blame anyone else but myself. You would think that at 49 years of age, there would be nothing else to learn about life. My mind goes slipping back to when I was twelve years old.

Mother always told me, "Don't go on the swing. Father has not fixed it yet." Did I listen? No. When I was eighteen years old, my family and friends said, "Don't get married. He is not the man for you."

What did I do? I married him, so life goes on, making one mistake after the other and never learning from my mistakes. I have two beautiful children who were taken from me. They said that I could not look after myself, let alone two children, and they were right.

I smoked and drank a lot. Things did not get any better. One morning, I found myself on the train. I looked out of the window, and for the first time, I really did take notice. The trees were so beautiful. I watched children waving as the train went by.

I looked at the little boy facing me. My hair had not been washed for days; he looked down at his feet and slowly looked back up at me. I turned away, ashamed.

My mind had stopped wandering. As I sat there looking through the window, I knew things had to change. I stood up, went to the toilet and washed my face and hands. I tidied my hair just as the train pulled into the stop.

As I placed my foot on the last step, I looked around and thought for the first time - *this is a brand-new day.* I left the train station and started walking down the lane.

Just then, an elderly gentleman tapped me on my shoulder and asked, "Would you like a lift?" He said, "Knowing that it is two miles to the town and you being a stranger." He looked at me and smiled.

I smiled back and said, "Thank you for the offer." The car was a very old one. I was surprised when I got into it and how comfortable it was. The old gentleman said with a grin, "It is leather, you know." I just looked at him.

He was busy talking to me about his wife. He said that he had lived without her for the last three years. "I was hoping to join her." I laughed and said, "Not yet." He replied, "No, not yet. I still have to feed the cat and pick up my laundry." We both laughed together.

From nowhere, I heard the screeching of brakes as I saw a truck coming towards us. There was nowhere for us to go. I remember thinking the truck was *in trouble.* I heard a scream; the screaming was coming from me. I felt myself being thrown out of the car and into the bushes.

I managed to crawl out, but every bone in my body was hurting. I found the old gentleman, but he was dead. I lay back and thought that was the nicest thing that had ever happened to me for a long time, the old gentleman offering me a lift and treating me like a person.

I remember his smile. I remember everything he said as I lay waiting for my last breath.

13.   Nowhere to Go

Nowhere to go."I keep on hearing him repeating, "Nowhere to go." Where do I go? I don't know. Why doesn't someone come and tell me? I watch him slowly pick up a pebble, skimming it across the water. Picking up another pebble, the pebble bounces two-three times off the water.

Looking around, there is no one there. He keeps looking as if he is waiting for someone and then sits down. Sensing someone was standing behind him, he asked, "Have you come for me? "Yes, I told him.

Then I asked him, "How long have you been here?" "A long time ". He replied. "About ten years." He said. Standing there, I found myself standing in front of him. I looked at him, thinking he must have been three or four years old when he came here.

I think he is reading my thoughts, and he replies, "No, five." We did not say anything for a long time; he just looked towards the water. The sun was setting, and it was getting dark. The boy stood up and started to walk towards the bushes. I ask, "Where are you going?" He looks back but says nothing. We did not speak anymore. He just kept walking away.

I sat there for a moment, looking at the water. It was some kind of a huge pond. It seemed to be shallow, but you could tell by the colour of the water that it went deep. It sent shivers up my spine. I was feeling very strange.

I got up and started to walk away. I could hear music, so I followed it to see where it came from. There was an old red truck parked with the radio blaring. I walked around, but there was nobody there. The truck was rusty and had quite a lot of dents. I looked in the back, and there were two or three old tyres in there.

As I looked in the front window, I saw an old checkered blanket on the front seat. It looked like a dog had been sleeping on it, as it was full of dog hairs.

The music was getting louder, so I placed my hands over my ears to keep out the noise.

What was happening - this was not me. He was taking me through his death with his eyes. I was going to feel everything that he felt. I found myself starting to walk, then run. I had a strange feeling that someone was running after me.

Panic started to take hold, and I found myself running. Then I felt someone grab my hair and pull me down, shouting all the time, "You bastard!". He just kept punching me until there was nothing left to punch. He stood up and wiped the blood from his mouth. It was all over his shirt and trousers, and his hair was dripping with blood - not his - mine.

I stood there looking at him, slurring his words and falling backwards. I looked down and could see myself there. I just could not believe what I was seeing as I watched him stagger back to the truck and come back with a bottle.

He sat beside me, his eyes blazing, and told me it was my fault. He kept pulling on my shoe, trying to pull me towards him. He stood up and fell backwards again. I stood beside him, looking at him.

I don't know how long I stood there, but it felt like a long time. I watched him stand up, still holding the bottle. I saw him walk to the truck and pick up a shovel. He started to dig. He kept digging, panicking, wiping his mouth, and swearing with every breath he took.

He pulled my battered body into the hole, covering me up and left me there. I couldn't think about anything - I just found myself waiting. I don't know why or what I was waiting for.

Then I was back. Telling you I've never seen you before. I saw you come over to me as I sat in the bushes. You told me to stand up, and as I stood, you started to talk to me about the dog.

I asked, "What dog?" and you told me to remember the dog. I stood there for a moment, and then I remembered I was taking my dog for a walk that day when the truck came around the corner. My dog ran out onto the road, and the truck went straight over him.

Screaming, I ran and picked my dog up. The man said, "Put the dog in the front seat, and he will take him to the vet." I would not let him take the dog without me, so I climbed in and placed the dog on the blanket. I don't know where we were going, but I remember seeing a sign saying, beware deer. We seemed to be going further into the country, but then we stopped. I shouted, "Where are we going? We have to get the dog to the vet."

His hand came down and hit me on my head. I watched him pull the dog out and drop him on the floor. Then he grabbed me by the scruff of my neck and pulled me out. That is when I started to run, but he soon caught up to me, dragging me through the bushes and beating me to death.

I closed my eyes and waited. After a time, a lady came to get me. She told me to trust her that she would look after us. As I let go of her hand, my dog came running towards me. That's when I knew it was all over, and we were both safe.

14. I Pulled the Trigger

I do not know much about anyone else. I just know about myself. If you ask me about the war, it was a waste of time and a waste of good lives. For what?

I grew up thinking of the good of mankind. What happens to all those mistakes people made in the name of wars and protecting their country?

What happened to all the millions of men who died protecting that thought? We have to feel that it was worth something to die for, and the question is,' Where do I go from here?

I am about to end my life, a life that I can no longer live. I looked down at the gun in my hand with no regrets about what I was about to do. I look to the sky and call out, "If there is a God, please help.

me." The only thought that came into my mind was about my friends who I had to leave behind on the battlefield.

I felt my hand squeeze the trigger. The music gets louder as I close my eyes, and tears fall down my cheeks. Was this the end?

This is his Story

What is happening to me? Your face fills my memories, but the memories only bring heartaches of a long time ago.

I had such dreams. I had not long left school when Mamma said, "It is best to stay a couple of years longer to get a good education." She was right. Mamma was always right. I can hear the clock ticking in the background as I remember the words I said to my Anna long ago.

The war had just begun, and I found myself one of those people who felt that they had to fight for their country. Yes, I did fight for my country, but I did not understand why. I just did it.

So many things were going on at that time. People I knew were lying dead at my feet. Today, I can still hear them screaming. I can still see my friends lying there, begging for someone to put a bullet through their heads so they do not have to suffer anymore.

Some of my friends just walk around in a daze, trying to understand what is happening. We were all confused young men who did not have the proper training to face what we had to face here.

When I came home, I did not walk into my mother's kitchen; someone had to push me in a wheelchair. I was not the same person who had left a long time ago. Now. I have no dreams of the future. I have left them back there.

My heartache as I let go of the girl I loved with all my heart. I never stopped loving her. Day after day, she would call and beg me to talk to her but I refused, until one day, she stopped calling. I heard that she had found herself a nice young man. I used to watch them walking around the town, hoping they would not see me.

I Pulled the Trigger

Damn the war! What else can it take away from me? Dear God, is this how my life is going to be? And close my eyes for a moment and you are there? Squeeze, my eyes closed tight, but the tears still come pouring through.

I heard someone screaming, someone calling for help. As the last thought comes into my mind, I see myself standing up from the wheelchair and walking towards a beautiful light. My friends are calling my name. As I proudly walk towards them, I turn around, and I am looking at someone in a wheelchair with a bullet hole in his head. There are no regrets.

My mates put their arms around my shoulder. At last, I feel a sense of belonging as we all talk at once. There is no looking back now, only looking forward to a lifetime of memories. Memories that will now stay in the past.

15. The Lost Puppy

I shouted, "Shoo!" The poor little thing went flying down the path, making funny noises as he hit his head on the wall. I went to pick him up, but he made a yelping noise that told me he was scared. I said, "I am so sorry, little puppy," bending down to pick him up.

He started to lick my cheek, and for the first time in nine months, I heard myself laughing again. As I held him in my arms, taking him inside, I looked through the window but could not see anyone outside. I thought tomorrow, I would ask the neighbour if she knew if the pup belonged to someone. In the meantime, what will I feed him?

Then fright took hold. I thought I must not get attached to this puppy. I don't want to lose anyone else. I quickly placed him back on the floor and went into the kitchen to see if there was anything I could give him to eat, but the cupboard was bare. I thought, what a nuisance, now I will have to go out and find him something to eat.

I did not want to go out, but I looked down at the little puppy, who was sitting there looking up at me. I put on my coat and went out the door and down the street.

I opened the door of the little corner store, and I noticed that the old gentleman who had always been there was not here today. There was a young man standing there looking very surprised.

He said, "Can I help you? My Dad had to go and pick Mom up, so they left me here." I smiled to myself and thought how uncomfortable he looked standing there. I said, "You will do fine.

What do puppies eat?" He looked at me and said, "I don't know." We both looked at each other, and then he smiled at me and said, "I remember seeing some cans with dogs on them. Maybe one of those will tell us." He went to where all the tinned food was kept. He brought three cans of different food for dogs.

He gave me two and said, "You read those, and I will read this." I took them from him, and we sat down on the boxes of potatoes and read the labels. Then he said, "I think this one will do fine. How old is your puppy?"

I said I did not know; he was very small. We both laughed together. He said, "I think this one will suit him fine. It says between one month and six months."

As I passed the money over the counter, I said, "We did very well, didn't we?" I asked him his name. He said his name was Derek. I said, "Pleased to meet you; my name is Paula." He smiled and said, "We did make a good team, didn't we?" I said "Yes." and walked home. When I got to the front door, I heard a whimper, and once again, I remembered the little puppy.

I had to shove the door open with him behind it. I thought I hoped I did not hurt him, but he did not seem to mind. He just latched onto my feet while I was trying to walk to the kitchen. He did make me laugh.

I opened the can, found a dish and placed it in front of him. He was straight into it. It was all over the floor and all over his face. He looked up at me with such a funny look. I bent down and picked him up. It was nearly bedtime. I thought I would put him in the kitchen and close the door.

I could hear him whimpering, and then he stopped. I was woken by something being caught in my hair. I jumped up, and it was the puppy. I wondered how he got out of the kitchen when the door was closed. I walked slowly back to the kitchen and was surprised to see the door still closed. I thought I must have left the door open last night and thought no more of it.

For the next few days, I placed a notice in the corner shop saying, *Found Puppy.* I asked the neighbours up and down the street, and I think they were very surprised to see me out and about. I had to carry the puppy because I was afraid he would run off and get hurt.

Three weeks passed, and no one came to claim him. By that time, I had gotten used to my new friend. He was so funny. I sat back in my chair and remembered one of my children saying, "Can we have a puppy, Mummy?" I said, "Yes, darling, but not yet."

Then, one day, I woke up and heard a lot of banging in the kitchen. I quickly got out of bed, and as I opened the kitchen door, I saw a ball being shoved gently over to the puppy. I watched the little dog go towards something - I was not sure what.

The Lost Puppy

I sat back and watched him. He sat back on his hind legs, front paws in the air and licked something, but there was nothing there. I could not understand how he was staying in that position. He looked so happy, and then the game started again. I watched the puppy play.

I watched the ball, and I watched him sit on his hind legs. I swear I heard my two children laughing. The tears came running down my face. To think that my children had come home. A little puppy brought them to me. I do not know how long they will stay, but I tell them every day that when they are ready to go, I will understand.

For now, I love to wake up in the morning and look forward to a brand-new day.

16. It Was The Bed, You See

I am never quite sure what stories I will write, but I always have plenty of people waiting to tell their stories.

Most of the time, I have a backlog of stories waiting to be written. I just need to jot down the title, and then I can come back and finish it later.

It was a Tuesday afternoon, and I was tuning into one of those people who had been waiting for a couple of days. Instead, I found someone completely different waiting.

I never refuse entry when someone comes as strong as she did. I knew this person needed help. But today, the lady was in too much of a hurry to wait any longer. Who could blame her as she had been waiting a long time to see her daughter Katie again?

It was the bed, you see. I kept hearing the same words repeatedly, asking, "What bed?" I asked

"The bed." She replied, looking at me with a strange look. "I am so sorry," I said, but I could not see anything. She smiled at me and said, "Shall we look together? Come here and sit on the bed beside me." I gently sat on the bed beside her, and then something happened; strange colours kept turning around in my thoughts: blues, reds, oranges, greens, purples. I asked myself, *what's going on?* From nowhere, someone said, *be patient.*

Then I heard her again. This was my daughter's bed, you know." I just looked and smiled. Before I could ask her name, she said her name was Katie. I watched her stroking the bed cover on the bed with so much love. She looked at me and asked, "When does the pain go away?" I did not say anything.

She clasped her hands together and said, "I wanted you to know. She never came." Still, I could not say anything. I watched as the tears started to fall as she searched for her handkerchief in her pocket. As she reached the bedside cabinet, I noticed, for the first time, a picture of a young girl.

I sat perfectly still, not daring to breathe incase I disturbed the moment. She took hold of the photograph and held it to her chest. "Do you believe in God?" she asked. I still could not answer. She said, "There was a time when I believed in God, but no more."

As she placed the photograph back on the bedside cabinet, I watched her stand up I noticed for the first time the door with the coats hanging on the back. She took one of the coats and placed it around her shoulders. In the next breath, she asked, "Are you ready?" I followed her down the stairs and out into the street.

It was early evening, and the sun was just going down. I did not ask where she was going I just followed.

When she stopped, I thought I heard a lot of children laughing. She looked at me, then looked away. I was looking at about eight to ten children playing in the street, all laughing at once.

Then everything seemed to get dark, and I sensed something was wrong. I just knew it was a strange feeling of nothing to see and nothing to feel, just emptiness. I felt myself praying to God to get me out of this. I heard someone whisper, *hold on, hold on*. The next moment, I was climbing the stairs leading to the same room.

As I opened the door once again, I saw the same person sitting on the bed. "Did you see her?" she asked. Her eyes were full of pity. "Please, did you see her? Katie was my daughter."

I didn't have time to think but the words came tumbling out, "Yes, I saw Katie." She stood up and ran towards me and asked, "Where?"

I said, "Waiting." "Waiting where?" She looked past me towards the door. Not daring to take my eyes off her face, I asked, "Do you remember that special place you used to take Katie?" She said, "Yes." I looked into her eyes and said, "She is waiting there."

All of a sudden, she let go of me, pushed me away, and ran down the steps out of the door and into the street. I took a deep breath and thought, *what happened*? Then, without questioning it anymore, "Yes, I did see what happened to Katie." Katie was a beautiful child and eager to please, so when this man came and asked her for help because there was a little puppy stuck in a shed, she could not say no.

17. Who Will Save My Children?

I am dying, but who will look after my children? The year is 1954, and I have five children, who are 11 to 3 years old.

I sit here everyday thinking, Will *tomorrow be my last day? Who will protect my children*? My mind goes back to the farmhouse and the Saturday evening dance.

That week was the first time I had been given permission to go to the dance. I could not believe my ears as I had a very strict upbringing in everything I did. My friend Emily and I grew up together in a small town. My father was a preacher and very strict, but Emily could twist him around her little finger.

When he finally gave in, she promised him that her older brother would come and pick me up, and the rule was to be home by 10 pm.

I was so excited, and when the evening came, father examined me from top to toe. He did not have to say anything to me because I just knew what he was thinking. I kissed him on the cheek as the car pulled into the drive. I could not let my father see the excitement that I felt. I was so excited as the door closed that I screamed out with excitement, running to the car. Billy, Emily's brother, asked if I was okay.

I just smiled as we took off down the road and round the bend. He said that he wanted to take me to his home first before we go to the dance. I didn't say anything. When we arrived at his home, Emily was there to meet us. She was so excited, taking hold of my hand and dragging me upstairs.

"Look what I have got for you." she said, with a huge grin, "a beautiful dress." It was the most beautiful dress that I had ever seen.

"I can't wear that," I said. "Oh yes, you can," Emily said. Before I knew it, she dragged my dress off and placed the other one on the top of my head, pulling it down around my waist and telling me not to look in the mirror until she finished.

When I did look, I couldn't believe the person looking back at me. *Was that really me? I wasn't a young girl anymore - I was a young woman.* She quickly put my hair up on the top of my head with a beautiful bone clip. "Smile," she said as she put some lipstick on my lips. I shot a glance at her and asked, "What will father say?"

She smiled and asked, "Are you going to tell him?" I looked in the mirror and said, "No."

We arrived at the dance, which was not glamorous - it was an old building, but to me, it was a palace. As the night went on, I was so afraid someone would ask me to dance because I didn't know how to dance, so I hid behind a wall.

A boy came from nowhere and grabbed my hand, saying, "I will show you how to dance." I said,

"No, thank you." I looked down at my shoes as he pulled me onto the dance floor. He held me so tight that I could hardly breathe, but I didn't care - I was so happy. His name was Philip, but everyone called him Phil.

After that night, we fell in love and became inseparable. Philip asked my father for my hand in marriage, but he said over his dead body.

Six months later, we were married, and our first child was born three months later. We did not have much, but we were happy. One day, Philip came home and said he was going to look for another job where he could earn more money. He left two days later and never came back.

They told me it was a train accident; he was trying to jump on the train when his foot slipped, and he fell under the wheels.

Who Will Save My Children?

It was very lonely without Philip, not just the money but also knowing that he would never walk through the door again, but life goes on.

I used to take washing in and do house cleaning jobs, just to keep food on the table. We were living in the hills, far from anyone or anything.

Then I got sick; it was a time when work was scarce, and money was even scarcer. Not many people had money, so we exchanged what we had. I had to travel down to the city, and most of the time, I had to leave my children on their own.

I used to sleep in the woods not far from the town because I did not have money for somewhere to stay. One day, the doctor said that I would have to go to the hospital, that I would be there for at least three weeks and that there was not much more they could do for me, that it was just a matter of time. I thought, *who would look after my children*?

Who Will Save My Children?

A woman from the city came and said she would pick up the children in two days' time. She said that I was not a fit mother to keep them and that she would find foster homes for them. I begged her to please let me keep my children.

I could hear the children in the other room crying. When she left, I told the children to sit at the table as I had something to tell them. I told them I would never leave them and how much I loved them all.

I made the best meal that we had ever eaten that night, laughing and singing together.

When the children finally went to bed, my oldest daughter said, "Please, mother, don't send us away." I looked at her and took her in my arms. As I did, I looked up to the top shelf where I used to keep the special bottle. I cradled her face in my hands and asked, "Are you sure you do not want to stay?" She understood what I was saying.

Who Will Save My Children?

We sat and talked for most of the night, and when the children got up the following morning, my daughter and I made a pot of tea. We spent the last moments talking about their father. One by one, the children started to fall asleep.

We both looked at each other and started to carry them one by one into my bed. Holding on to each other, I turned the radio on and sang to my children while they fell asleep. Then, I checked on my oldest child. Are you ready?'' I asked her. "yes, Mother'' she said and took hold of my hand.

We both closed our eyes and fell asleep. Most of you would not agree with what I did. I look back now with all that guilt.

Could I have done any better? Could I have done things differently? You have to live in the time and place where I grew up to understand.

I was so afraid to leave my children behind, not knowing if they would have been kept together.

143

Knowing what I did, did I make the right choice? I have gone through so much guilt.

Was I running away from life? I do not know, but I have been wandering around for a long time now without my children. I thought I could hear them calling me. I am so tired. I would like to see my children again. Then I feel a woman standing beside me, holding my hand, telling me to trust her.

I close my eyes, thinking everything will be fine now. When I opened my eyes again, I felt the children once more in my arms. This time, I am not going to let them go.

18. Feathers

Do *you remember the times, places and schools that you attended all those years ago? I look back, and the memories come flooding in the times when you think you'll never make friends – that you will never fit in and nobody will like you. How does time change so quickly, and does life really pass us by, or do we pass life by?*

Sometimes, we go forward, and sometimes, we stay all our lives in the same place, but our memories will always stay with us.

Could it be my imagination, or is this for real? I stepped back and looked again - two children playing pillow fights. The memories came flooding back: the school, the place, and my beautiful friend. Oh, what memories we had. I cried all the way to the train station and cried even more when my mother put me on the train. I hated the thought of leaving my friends behind to attend a new school.

The train took an hour to arrive. In between times, I stuck my nose in the window because I was determined not to talk to anyone. There was a girl sitting in front of me with a grin on her face. I said, "Do you mind?" She replied, "Not if you do not." I looked away again. Once again, I thought I was not going to like this place.

The train came to a grinding stop, and it was time for me to get off. I took my cases down and waited until most of the people got off the train. Then I heard a male's voice calling *Jenny Colette* and *Jenny*

146

Colette again. I thought, heck, everyone will know my blooming name by now. I waved to the gentleman, hoping that people would not look, but he was calling my name again. This time, I will have to walk up to him.

He took my baggage, put them in the back of his car and said, "I am pleased to meet you." I grunted and climbed aboard. It was only a few moments before we arrived at the front of the school.

Oh boy, was it big? The gentleman said, "We're here, Miss." As I stepped down from the car, for just one moment, I felt lost. Then, the girl who I had met on the train walked past me and said, "Are you sure you can find your own way there?" With a smirk in her voice, she turned away, and I stuck my tongue out at her.

I'd already climbed the stairs and gone through the big front door when the lady in front of me said, "Hurry child, hurry child." and I was guided through another door to what looked like twenty beds all in a row.

Guess what? The same girl was there again. "Can you find your way to the bed?" she said, with another smirk on her face. "Yes," I said and thought, *your time will come*. After settling in and trying to find my way around, it was now bedtime. Tomorrow will be another day, I thought.

I settled into the school better than I thought. I was getting used to the hustle and bustle. Funnily enough, I started to like Lila, the girl on the train. We started to enjoy each other's company and quickly found two other girls - one was Annette, who was from America. Oh, boy, was she fun. She taught us to smoke. The other girl was very slim and was from Canada. We would do everything together and were always sent to the headmistress for misbehaving.

What a time we had! The worst time was the Christmas that we spent together and the sadness of leaving one behind when the other two had to go home for the holidays.

I was just thinking the other day when I received a letter from Annette's husband - *I'm sorry to inform you that Annette has passed away.*

I slowly slipped the letter into my pocket; I was surprised to remember that she would now be seventy-two years old and I myself was seventy-one.

I have not heard from Lila for a year now. The last I heard was that she was in some kind of old people's home. Oh, the memories! I waved to the children in the window. You see, I knew everyone; I never left the school.

19. Our Last Farewell

I stood there listening to three young girls laughing and talking about the factory where they all worked.

I heard one of them saying, "Only two months to go, and we'll have enough money." They were still laughing when one of them said she had already saved her money. They seemed to have been pooling their money together to buy something.

I was not quite sure of what, but there were three happy young girls standing there, and that was all that mattered.

One of the girls said, "I have to go now. I have to pick mum up." The other two girls waved as she turned to the next street. What do these three girls have in common, and why did their lives change so much? Where in the future does destiny take us? Do we really know? Standing there waving. I looked up at the big boat and saw my two friends. I thought to myself *that it should have been me.* I waved to them until I could not see them anymore. I took a deep breath and walked back to the gate. The taxi driver said, "Is everything okay, love?" I said, "Yes, thank you." and climbed into the taxi.

Before I got to my stop, I asked him, "Please stop the taxi. He Stopped. I thanked him, gave him his fare and watched him as he drove away. I walked towards the park. I always enjoyed going there. I sat and fed the ducks with their little ones.

I thought of all the months that I had saved so desperately hard - we all had. My friends and I had found a newspaper clipping advertising the holiday of a lifetime. We talked about it for months and then decided we would all go together - it would be cheaper that way. We could put two or three into the sleeping quarters to save money. We were very excited.

I worked extra shifts at the factory, as did all my other friends. It was getting close to 12th March. We did not spend anything; we saved every penny we could. We all decided that we would do each other's hair and swap clothes so we did not have to buy anything new.

We enjoyed it just the same, which cut the shopping bill down by half. A week before the ship sailed, my mother got sick. She begged me to go, but I was afraid that something might happen while I was away. I knew I would never forgive myself.

So here I am, as usual, feeding the birds and feeling sorry for myself. I walked across the park to my mother's basement flat. It was London, and it was always difficult to get cheap accommodation, so we had the bottom flat.

It felt like it was underground; there were no windows, only two doors - one at the back and one at the front.

Mother was still in the hospital, so I quickly changed my clothes. The hospital was only ten minutes away, and when I got there, she looked so ill. The doctor shook his head as he walked by. I knew what he was trying to tell me.

Mother had consumption. The doctor said it was caused by damp places and not enough good food when she was younger. She recognised me straight away and tried to lift her hand and wave to me, but she was too weak. I sat beside her and told her about my friends.

She said that she was so sorry that she could never forgive herself. I said I would not have enjoyed the trip knowing that she was sick. She grabbed my hand so tightly and said, "Promise me, Lela, that you will leave the flat as soon as you can." She held my hand so tight I did not know where she got the strength from. I looked into her eyes and said, "I promise." She looked again and said, "Don't wait too long, and promise me that." I promised, and in the next second, she was gone. I sat there, not believing what had just happened - how she could have gone so quickly.

It must have been an hour later when the doctor walked by and looked in. "Is everything all right, Lela?" I looked at him and said, "I think she's gone." He quickly called a nurse, and she pulled the curtains around and said, "Why didn't you call? We thought you were just waiting for her to wake up." I looked at them in a daze and said, "I suppose I was."

Things got a bit hectic after that as I slowly walked away. I opened the door of the flat, looked around and really saw the flat for the first time. It was damp, dark and dingy, and Mother was right. I thought about the promise I had made and thought about how I could ever get the money to move out of here. I walked into her bedroom, sat on her bed and cried myself to sleep. The following morning, I got up, dressed and walked out into the fresh air.

The milkman asked if I had heard from my friends yet. I said, "Don't be daft; they've only been gone two days." He smiled and handed me the milk. I walked to the markets to pick up some bread and cakes. I always got my mother a cake.

She loved cakes. I had already paid for it when I thought Mother was *not here anymore.* Tears came flooding, and one of the storeholders, Hanna, came, put her arms around me and said, "I'm sorry about your mother. She was a good woman."

I said, "I'm so sorry. That was silly of me." She took my hand and said, "Let's go have a cup of tea." She asked me if I had any other relatives. I said, "No." but we did have somebody in Bath. She said, "Where the hell is that?"

I said I did not know, but I thought my mother's sister was somewhere. I thought for a moment and then remembered the letter that Mother had received one Christmas. I thanked her, dried my tears and walked out. I went back to the hospital. One of the doctors was waiting for me. He asked what I would like to do with my mother's remains.

I said I did not know. He said not to worry that he would send someone to see me in the next couple of days to organise the funeral. He asked if I knew whether Mother had any money for a funeral. I said, "Yes, she had a policy." He said, "That is good news." and walked away.

I went back to the flat again and thought I had a better check and made sure that I had enough money to bury her. I looked through all the paperwork and could not find anything, but then I remembered the Christmas box. Mother used to call it the Christmas box because she saved extra pennies to make sure we had something for Christmas.

I found it on top of the wardrobe. I was very surprised to see so much paperwork in there, but I found the book. I turned the pages and was surprised at the money that Mother had saved. The final count was £400.00. I could not believe it. I wondered how she managed to save so much money.

She worked all her life, but we never had much. Why did she save so much money? I thought of all the times she went without many things. I remembered her words: *leave the flat.* I did not tell anyone about the money. The following day, someone came from the hospital and asked if I had enough to cover the expense of the funeral. If I did not, they could put her in a pauper's grave. I said, "No, thank you, my mother is well provided for." and held my head up high.

He gave me some addresses of funeral places; I put my hat on and walked down the street. The first

157

one was a very small man, who I took an instant dislike. However, I thanked him and walked out. The next one was a nice lady, and we sat and talked. We ordered the coffin and the headstone.

She asked if there was anyone to walk behind the coffin. I said, "No, only me." She asked me if I would mind if she walked alongside. I told her I would be very grateful.

The funeral went very well. Mother would have loved it. I bought white lilies to put on top. I could hear her say, "*Don't spend too much money on me. Keep it for yourself.*" I smiled to myself.

It was going into the second week when I opened the local newspaper. It said all on board were killed; their ship had been accidentally torpedoed. I thought, *what is a torpedo boat doing in the middle of the Atlantic Ocean?*

I thought of our last farewell; my friends were looking so happy, waving, and looking forward to a great holiday. Where were they now? The 6 pm news had just started as I turned on the radio. It stated that a ship had been called out in the early hours after an SOS was put out. The ship had already been sunk with all hands on board.

I waited for news, but it took a long time to come. Then it stated that if there was reasonable doubt that the ship had been fired on without just cause, then we would be at war. I caught my breath and thought, *how sad to have lost my friends and thought how lucky I was.*

I remembered my mother's words and thought; *it is time for me to go.* I found her sister's letter and decided to go to Bath. As I climbed onto the train once more, I thought of my mother. I could see her smiling at me, saying, Well done, girl.

20. That Ring

Just when we give up on life and think nothing matters anymore, someone taps us on the shoulder and says, "Wake up; it's time to remember."

When I first met the two women, they were looking in two huge bins behind a shopping centre. I thought one of them would fall in, but you could see that they were used to leaning into the bins. You could hear them telling each other what they had found. I heard a loud bang every time they closed the bin lid down and smiled to themselves.

As I looked at both women, my heart went out to the - two ladies in ragged clothes. One pushed a pram; the other one was pushing a shopping trolley. Both of them didn't notice I was standing there. It started to rain. This is their story.

That Ring

Here I am again, trying to find another meal, and night after night, I would go to the shop bins for food. I lifted up the third bin lid, which is normally my lucky bin, but today it is empty. I've been looking in these bins for the past five years. I was talking to my friend last night, and she told me that they are not going to put food into the outside bins and that there have been too many problems with people fighting to get there first.

I have to go and see old Charlie at the fish and chip shop to see if he can spare me a small feed. He is pretty good, but he does not like you to come too many times. I can understand that. I look around and see old Mary coming towards the bins; I tell her I have checked them. There is no food tonight.

She said she was hoping to get something to eat because she had not eaten at all that day. I took hold of her hand and told her we would try the fish and chip shop.

Mary lost her teeth a long time ago, so she finds it difficult to chew. We have spent quite a few nights together huddled up, trying to keep warm; every year, I think it will be her last, but she keeps on going.

I see Charlie outside the fish and chip shop, and he says, "Well, ladies, what can I do for you tonight?" He knows I would not ask him if I did not need his help. He told us to go to the back door and that he would find something for us. He knows me, as Charlie and I have been going back for a long time. If I remember correctly, it would be 25 or maybe 26 years.

Things were different then. I was married with two children and had my own house and money in the bank, all because of a bloody ring. It was September, and we'd just picked the girls up from school. My husband David was late as usual picking us up. I remember saying to him that he was always late and that he would be late for his own funeral.

For some unknown reason, David flew into a rage while he was driving, took off his wedding ring and threw it out of the window. I told him to pull over. I got out of the car, slammed the door and walked back to look for the ring. Within seconds, a truck came around the corner and hit the car head-on.

There was not much left of the car, and David and my lovely children were gone. The truck seemed to swallow the car up and everything in it. I could not believe what I was seeing. I heard David shout out my name, and that was the last time I heard his voice. Sometimes, when I sleep, I hear David calling me. I put my hands over my ears to try and drown out the sound. It seems such a long time ago. I waved goodbye to old Mary and slowly walked away.

That Ring

Walking towards the river, where it was so peaceful, I remember the old bridge where David and I first met. Our first kiss, *oh God, what did I do*? I blame myself for causing the argument. I see the scene played over in my mind - the car, the truck, and David pulling off his ring, then watching the ring fly out of the window.

My head hurts now because I am trying to stop the visions. Once more, I take out my bottle. I have never stopped drinking that day, and the drink is no longer helping me forget.

I look up to the middle of the bridge, and my eyes quickly fall on a young girl climbing onto the railings. I drop everything and run like hell. My heart is pounding, and I am thinking I am not going to make it.

Just as I get there, she falls over the side. Without thinking, I jump in straight after her. The sharp, cold water brings my senses alive deeper and deeper I go.

I think I must get rid of some of my clothes; I am used to wearing extra clothes and keeping all my belongings in huge pockets. I take off my coat and am still trying to bring my senses into focus. *Where is she?* I open my eyes and look around, and I can see her just below me. I turned around and dived deeper. Grabbing hold of her shoulder, I start to pull her up. I am losing my breath and wonder if I am going to make it.

I grab onto her clothes even tighter and think, "*Please, God, let me save at least one life.*" I see my husband and hear him calling me. He's telling me that everything is going to be ok. As my head breaks through the surface, I drag her up against my body. I quickly slap her around the face. She opens her eyes, coughing and spluttering, gasping for breath.

I hear a police car and see people coming down to the embankment. I shove her onto the rocks, and then something shimmering in the water catches my eye. I look again, *yes, it is the ring.* I quickly push myself out to where I can see something shining. I still have a little further - just a little more. I reach out, pick it up and then feel a sense of relief. I hold the ring tightly in my hand and think it is over.

I feel something tugging at my clothes and then feel a bump on my head. Something has hit me; it was a boat. I must have been too far out. I could not see anything. What is happening? Still grasping the ring in my hand, I hear my husband calling my name. I see him and hold my hand out to him.

I shout at the top of my voice, "I have your ring." I hold my hand up so that he can see the ring, and then I feel the warmth of his hand. He is telling me that everything is ok. As he slowly pulls me up, I feel the warmth coming into my body and the love all around me. Once again, I stand by my husband's side. I open my hand and say, "See, I found the ring."

21. The Souls That Wait

Now, that is something I can talk about. When I sit at my computer and start a story, I look around, and I can see a woman sitting there fiddling with 4 to 5 pieces of paper; her story is about letters.

The woman sitting on the chair fiddling with the ring and the locket were other stories. The woman was standing by the side of me, holding out her hand and showing me the locket, telling me how beautiful she thought the locket was.

A man is sitting in the corner in a wheelchair with a gun in his hand' looking down at it and then looking back at me. I Pulled the Trigger

I knew I had to listen to his story next. Every story that I write is written by automatic writing.

My house is always full of beautiful souls waiting to tell their stories, and I see more and more every day.

I have learned one important thing - the spirit world still loves to come back and communicate in any way they can. Some of them have found the door to my living room - just to be there for that moment of time, to tell me their story. I am very grateful that they chose me. Once they have left, they want to come back and live through their experiences once more.

22. Sylvia

I could hear my sister calling me, "Sylvia, come on." I looked up at the window towards the red shoes. They are so close. I thought if I could only reach them. I could still hear my sisters calling me as I looked back at the red shoes.

They were so beautiful. I tried to stretch my hand out to reach them. Turning around, I could just faintly hear my sisters calling me again.

I thought I heard an explosion. I could hear my sisters crying and calling to each other, and I could feel the pain. It was so bad that I could not breathe. The shop where my red shoes were was all but gone. Only the red shoes were left there in the window, or was it my imagination? I felt my sister Sarah trying to pull me closer to her. I looked back towards the window to the red shoes and thought of all the times that I had walked past the window, looking at the beautiful red shoes.

I used to stand there for hours just admiring them. On each of the red shoes was a beautiful black bow, and in the centre of the black bow was a beautiful diamond. My sisters used to laugh at me, saying, "They are not real diamonds. They are just a shiny stone." But to me, they were diamonds.

I had four sisters, and I was the youngest. That meant that when their clothes did not fit them anymore, they would be passed down to me. When I went to school, the girls would laugh at me, saying, "You've got Mary's skirt on, and that is Sarah's top."

Mother tried very hard to feed and clothe all of us; life wasn't easy for any of us. My Father passed away when I was four years old. Mother said it was a coughing fever. A lot of my mother's and father's friends died the same way.

Sylvia

My sisters were very protective of me - always trying to help me with my schoolwork, but I hated school. I used to dream about red shoes every day. I thought if I owned those red shoes, my life would change.

I could feel the red shoes getting further and further away now. I thought I could hear Sarah talking to me, but I could not see her. From nowhere, I heard my father's voice asking fairly quietly, "Do you really want those red shoes, Sylvia?"

I heard myself saying, "Yes, I really do want those red shoes." Father then asked me, "Do you remember when you were a little girl and you used to play dress-up with your sisters? You were always the first one to find your mother's best shoes. Your mother tried to hide them from you in case you fell over and hurt yourself. They were miles too big for you, but you loved wearing them."

I remember my sisters and I playing house. We would take Mother's shoes from the closet and a couple of her dresses, and we would pretend to be grown-ups with a broom and an old curtain hanging over our heads. I used to think *what a wonderful world that was.*

I remember thinking *that was the best time of my life.* As I remember, my father loved all of us very much and never said a crossword to any of us. We were all happy when Father was home. Just before he died, he asked us all to look after Mother. That we would all have to be strong people now and look after each other.

He explained that he would have to go away, but he did not want to go, telling each and every one of us how much he loved us once again.

We were all looking forward to Christmas, and I'm sad to say that my father never made it. He died just before Christmas. I look back again to where the red shoes were. Once again, I could not reach them. I heard my sisters laughing, and as I looked, I saw my sisters playing dress up; this time, Sarah had red shoes on. She asked me, "Do you like my red shoes? I just looked.

I wanted to go towards my sister, take the red shoes from her, and put them on my feet, but something was stopping me. Then I heard a voice telling me to let go of the red shoes and to let go of the memories of the red shoes.

I looked back, but the shoes were no longer sitting in the window. I looked towards where I heard my sisters laughing, and I saw the red shoes in front of her. My sister shouted, "Come on Sylvia, come and get your red shoes." All I could think of was the red shoes. I stood up and felt myself walking towards the red shoes.

Then I felt my sisters all around me, telling me that they had been waiting for me, that there had been a gas explosion and the entire street had been blown up.

Still holding on to the red shoes, I saw the woman waving to me and remembered her telling me to let go of the red shoes, but I held them even tighter in my arms. Then she told me something I would never forget as I slowly let go of the red shoes.

23. Thomas

Thomas asked." can you see me? Yes. 'I told him at this moment, I can. What," are you doing here? He asked. I am going to have my eye fixed. What for, he asked? I have cataracts in both eyes, 'what for,' he asked again.

Then he looked over to the other side of the room. I see you got to see him he said, "Who I asked? The man himself" Oh God, No, I said. Looking over to see my friend Fred standing there. I asked do you know my friend Fred No." not really. But," I have heard about him. 'Leaning over,' whispering in my ear, then looking away." saying.' I have to go now," someone is calling me."

I asked him if he had come to visit someone. No," he said; most of them I see are unconscious. I just looked at him," coming back to stand by my side, he said the soul wonders, and sometimes, they can get a bit confused; that is where I come in.'' I talk to them,' while they sleep and keep them grounded.

Well, now he said   I must go now. See you later, he said, and he was gone.

I lay back in my bed and waited. Then I heard someone say, '' Has he gone? Yes, I said; he is so bossy, you know. But he is very good.

I just looked at her.'' she was different; her blue hair stood in the air, with a huge bow on one side. I will walk with you to where they will be operating on you, and then I must go.'' Thames will be there waiting; he is "always,'' waiting. She said.

The nurse came in and asked me my name and date of birth, and then I was wheeled straight into the theatre; they told me that the operation would not take long and that I would be aware of what was going on all the time. I did not feel anything.

'I could hear someone talking all the time. 'Saying Ho.'' he is good.'' you know. Then I felt someone standing by the side of me. He does a beautiful job. He said. Then asked me what I felt.' I told him nothing. All I could see was a light, 'I told him.' you're not going to the light yet,' he said with a smile.'

After a while, I heard someone say, it is finished. Good. Thames said with a smile. I never felt a thing he said, tapping on the shoulder and smiling.'' I said me neither. And he was gone.

The operation was successful, and I was wheeled back into the ward. I had made a fantastic new friend while I was waiting to go into surgery, and I hoped that one day we would meet again.

Now I am waiting to get the other eye done.'' I was told it would be at least three months. But what a wonderful world.'' I thanked Thames for being there with me until the operation had finished.

I know now. 'That he was holding my hand all the time, and he never left my side until the job was finished.

While I lay there, I saw Thomas running past. Did you see her? He asked. No," I am sorry I did not, I shouted, but he was long gone.

It is strange about the timing, by the time. I closed my eyes maybe a second later. Thomas had already completed his journey of finding the person that he was looking for,' then taken them back safely before they awoke, saying that there is always one" that tries to get away with a grin." but I always get my man. Thomas said," and he was gone.

It is always good to know. Someone is always waiting to help," from either side, no matter where they are or what I do. There is always someone waiting.

24. Annabelle

I was talking the other morning to my friend on the phone. When all of a sudden someone crept from behind me, I had to stop my friend for talking for a moment. I did not want to lose the little girl she was only about seven out scraggy blondish hair, wearing a strange dress her arms and feet were dirty and her nose running.

I tried to say something but she vanished again. It was not until the afternoon, I was sitting down looking at the new seeds that I had bought. I looked up and there she was again. She came and stood behind me, what are you doing she asked me? Thinking. What about she asked? I suppose lots of things, she stood there for a moment in thought. She came and stood in front of me I could see her more plainly. She picked up the end of the dress, started to turn it around, and around screwing the corner tighter and tighter until the back of the dress was pulling on the back of her legs still talking away turning the piece of material over and over again. Do you have a name? I asked. She thought from a moment and said, Annabelle.

That is a beautiful name. I told her, they don't call me Annabelle she said looking straight into my eyes and leaning forward to touch the necklace that I wore around my neck. What do they call you? Ann. Anna, sometimes, depending on if they get cross with me. I leaned towards the table to put my cup down turnaround, and she was gone. I waited for the moment but she did not come was 2:45. Now my eyes are getting tired, so I decided to lay on the bed. I laid down for a few minutes. When I saw young Annabelle again, standing by the side of the bed, are you sick? She asked concerned, no, I am just tired.

Climbing, into bed beside me she said with a big sigh. Yes, I get tired sometimes, she lay beside me, but I couldn't feel her. Will you sing to me? She said, would you like me to? Can you sing faraway places; I don't know that one. Never mind. I heard her take a deep breath, that's all I remember. I must have dropped off to sleep. When I woke up, she had gone. I just finished making my husband's tea. When I felt Annabelle standing by the side of me again...

Are you going, again she asked? Where, I asked? The place that you went the other day. She was trying to point somewhere but not making any sense. It was not until later that I realise what she was trying to tell me now.

I remember I was at Fair Bridge over a month ago and I met this little girl then but somehow her energy seemed different. It didn't seem like it was tied to one spot some strange. I know from appearances that sometimes a person cannot let go of the memory that has kept her there for such a long time. Now she has found a way to move the energy, she as connected to my memories Have you got a mommy, she asked me? Yes, I told her.

Do you remember your mommy? Yes, I told her. What do you remember? She said one of the friends that live with me, she said that she knew. My mummy. And that she was never going to come for me. I said she will come one day, she said she was dead. I asked her how she knew my mum was dead. She said everybody's mommy is dead. How do you know? Well, Flo told us. They were all dead and there was never can I come to get us.

What did you do during the day I asked? I wash dishes, she said. I would get on a crate and stand there and I could reach the sink and I would wash the dishes that was my job. Every day I would have to wash the dishes that is not a very good job she said looking at me, is it? Are you going to ask me to wash your dishes? No. I said. I will wash them later.

What would you like to do now? I looked to where she was standing but she had gone again.

Later that evening. My husband and I was watching the television, I felt Annabelle coming closely and sitting beside me whisper in my ear, is he going to stay all night Yes, I told her, then I shan't stay she said very loudly and she was gone. I felt I was trying to catch a butterfly. Maybe tomorrow, she would come back again.

25. My Books

My books will tell you all you need to know about life and Death and everything in between. They will connect you to your loved ones and tell you their story.

You will learn about the weepers, the souls that never rest. You will understand reincarnation, as well as how, why, and when. But most of all, you will know The Truth, The Whole Truth and Nothing But the truth From The spirit people themselves.

26. Comment on One of Your Stories

Hey Pam. So I will comment just as someone reading a short story. I have looked into automatic writing, but I'm afraid I lack the context or, I suppose, experience to make any deeper comments on that,

But I find the subject quite interesting. Just as a reader, I thought the prose was great. It had a "light as a feather" touch to it. The way you describe this young lady drifting through the halls of this purgatory realm is very striking.

When you described that she wanted to press the buttons but had this feeling she couldn't, I was really impressed. Such a tactile feeling, and very intriguing.

I also found this mentor character very intriguing. He was very helpful and almost so casual about the whole thing. I found all that very interesting, especially the short description of how ghosts can move objects by willing it to be so.

Which is a nice little description of poltergeist activity? It ties up nicely in the end with a beautifully written description of the young lady passing into the other side which I very much enjoyed.

In conclusion, it was a short, nice little glimpse into a world beyond ours that I found intriguing and left me with more questions that won't probably get answered, but that's part of the intrigue.

I wish I had more context in terms of automatic writing and how you felt when you wrote this story.

Do you simply get conveyed a story that you yourself have to write it? Or are the words imprinted into your head from somewhere else and you just record them?

Either way, I enjoyed this. No.' they are everywhere I go, but most of all they are here with me, waiting to tell me their stories, you see some people have not yet learned to let go of this world, through fear, or they do not want to leave their loved ones behind. They want to stay with them. That is a choice they make whether to go, or whether to stay.

I received the ones that decided to stay. Because once their loved ones have passed on. There is no reason for them to stay earthbound, so they want to let go now. And that is where I come in.

I have listened to more than 800 stories and I am still listening today.

The stories are very sad. And very much to the point each story only last 7 to 11 pages and in those pages. They tell me about their life here on earth and what they did. But mostly the reason why they stayed. Every story has a message in them for someone.

Like the little girl that died of cancer. She came back to tell me her story. Hoping that by listening to her side of the story. People would understand. And not fear to let their children go because both parties need to move on.

And it is difficult when we love someone so dearly. That we hold them back through love. I am on my 21st book now, but this book will be different. This book is about me and how I listen to their stories and how I got the gift of listening.

My work is called automatic writing. Some people call it channelling. If you know someone that can do what I do. I would be very grateful. Regards Pam McCagh.

27. Letters to Say Thank You

Dear Pam,

Thank you. You are the real deal; I thank you for giving me the opportunity to connect with my daughter, who passed last year.

I have been grieving immensely and have been asking her for a sign that she is ok. My mother spotted your advertisement, and I emailed you. You followed up with a call, which you channelled into energies straight away.

One of them was a man bringing forward a girl, who turned out to be my daughter. I believe the male was her late uncle, who passed away a few years prior. She kept a photo of him after his passing on her desk

. You described her so accurately that I knew that you were talking to her or sensing her energy. I am not sure how it works, but I knew it was her, and there was no way you would know these private details. I was able to get some answers that I was looking for, and my daughter was able to give me messages that she needed to.

It is something that you cannot put a price on for a mother who has lost a child, and I am a bit more at peace knowing those details, knowing that she is happy and being looked after by my family,

I am no longer in anguish because of our session. You have a gift, and that gift has given me something so precious that words could not even give it justice.

I recommend to any mothers out there who are alone, in pain from the grief, to contact Pam. Just to communicate with your child that you have lost helps tremendously. I feel blessed to have had that opportunity. Thank you so much, Pam. Kind Regards, Emma.

Nobody told me the pain would stay so long. Pammi,

Nobody told me how to hold on to him and that he would always be with me. Thank you for your phone call.

I can now feel that he will never leave me until we are both ready to let go. I love him so much, Pammi.

Since we last talked, my husband and I have plans to go away for a short trip. My husband is learning to live again also, and with your help and understanding, I know we will come through with Jami in mind and soul,

We thank you

I hope you don't mind me calling you Pammi.

Love Ruth.

28. Learning Things Day

I am learning things day by day about the other side and the people who live there. Every day for me is a new learning experience.

This story is one of those where sometimes we miss that connection for some reasonor other. I sometimes think we live life through experiences of life itself.

There is one thing for sure: love is the most precious gift God ever gave us. It is the only thing that puts excitement and dreams into our lives. It is the love, the touch, and the memories of the person we love that we come back for time and time again.

29. Comments

Comments to the author of the book The Gift From The American Readers. Book awards.

I have always been fascinated by books written on clairvoyance, mediums, and other topics related to conversing with spirits, and this book kept me and will keep all readers glued to it because of the topic. Not everyone can listen to spirits or hear their voices and the author uses her unique gift to convey many stories that will help readers realize that death is but a moment of time. The author has shared their stories with passion and dedication, that way giving a better perception about death. The stories will give readers the confidence to talk about living and dying and will encourage them to do so. This book will touch the hearts of readers in many ways because it is a book about memories of loved ones, their stories, loss, and love in lives, and about life and letting go. It also gives a peek into another dimension that exists beyond the human plane in a very interesting way.

Comment

Reviewed By Gisela Dixon

The Gift by Pam McCagh is a non-fiction book on Pam's paranormal experiences as a psychic. In this book, she mainly details her experiences as a medium while communicating with dead people. The Gift starts off with a short introduction to the topic and subject matter, and Pam explains her process. Her stories are through "automatic writing" or basically written as they came to her, whenever and however that might be. At such times, she is sometimes not even aware that she wrote certain things. This book contains many such stories of people who are no longer alive but talk to Pam either to share, question, confess, or just express feelings, their lives, their memories of both life and death, and more. There are also links provided to access more information by Pam in this book. Thank you for the gift of reading your book.

To my dear friend

I would like to take this opportunity to say thank you for bringing my wonderful husband along to see me.

There is not a day that has gone by that I have not missed him.   But with your kind words and understanding. I now know that my husband is safe.

You brought a new meaning to my life and an understanding I will never forget. But most of all, who taught me to believe that there is a life after death,

I talk to my husband every day now, and the loneliness has gone.

Once again, thank you to my dear friend, Pamela. I am Betty. The one with the roses.

To Pam

I am writing this letter, hoping that you will receive it. You have given me a new life to look forward to. You helped me come to terms with losing my daughter. I am so grateful for that. You told me that by holding on too tightly, I was not learning to let go. It did take a long time to let my little girl go.

You said take your time. It is strange that I feel my little girl around me more now than I ever did holding on to her. I have started to enjoy her company when I get up in the morning. I call out good morning. I looked out of the window, and I talked to my daughter, telling her that a new day had begun for both of us. That one day, we will all be together again and enjoy the time that we have now. You taught me that.

My life has changed now, and every day, I look forward to a new beginning. Thank you with all my heart. My brother also says thank you because he says I am a different person now. He knows that I can now cope with my life. Love to you and your family.

You are always in my heart.

Betty and Clive. England

I would like to say

Thank you

To my

My Husband Paul; Paul, my son;

And Jonathan, my friend

who helped me to put this book together.

And, of course, all the people who made

this book possible.

Sleep Never Comes: For Those That Did Not Reach the Other Side;

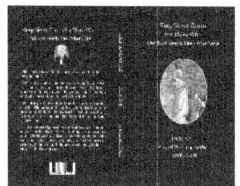

BOOK 1

A ward Winning Author

This Book Won A Medal And Also Five Gold Stars

Short Story - Non-Fiction

"Sleep Never Comes: For Those that Did Not Reach the Other Side" is a novel that comprises of many short stories by Pam McCagh, a gifted medium that communicates with the other world through Automatic Writing. The stories are not like any other short stories out there; they are stories told by people who exist between the living world and the hereafter.

Sleep Never Comes For Those That Did Not
Reach The Other Side Part 2

I'm sitting here thinking, how will I tell you about this book? There are so many spirit people involved that I feel very honoured to tell you some of their stories.

Where do I begin? I am a listener for the people on the other side. I don't want to change your ways of thinking or try to tell you something that you don't want to hear; I'm not here to do that, but I need to tell you.

The Truth,The Whole Truth And Nothing But The Truth. That there is life after Death, and a beautiful one at that. Pam McCagh. Copy Wright

Award-Winning Author,

Pam McCagh has just won her Second Medal.

Can Butterflies Cry?

Comments from the American **Book reviews**

Short Stories

The title is based on the story of a special girl named Mandy, psychic-medium, and author Pam McCagh continues her dictations of stories from the other side with Can Butterflies Cry through her gift of Automatic Writing. There are also personal stories from her childhood memories with her loved ones, her first encounter with the spirits, and her thoughts on her life as their interpreter.

The Whispering Souls

Award-Winning Author Pam McCagh

Comments from the American Book reviews

The stories told in The Whispering Souls are from departed ones made possible by author and medium Pam McCagh through her Automatic Writing. One aspect of the book that I love very much is Pam McCagh's personal journeys and important messages about life that we all could learn from and take as inspiration. Once you start, you can't read just one. They are like medications, healing soul-starved people in a precarious world that lacks spiritual enlightenment nowadays. These stories offer hope, courage, love, and motivation. They nourish the soul.

The caretaker of souls

I am the Soul Seeker, the Seeker of Souls, and I take souls across every day.

People come to me from all over the world and from all walks of life to tell me their stories; they tell me of their life and Death and past memories. I have listened to hundreds of stories, written 24, and won three awards in American books by Memories, Their Memories.

Some of the stories will break your heart. Some of them will stay with you forever, and some you will want to let go of. I am the Soul Seeker, the Seeker of Souls, and I am their storyteller.

Letter Of Hope.

A Letter Of Hope is about the beginning, the end and somewhere in between.

A Letter Of Hope is about the future and the past. It is about hope when you think you have nothing else to live for. But most of all, it is a cry for help. It is about waiting and hoping.

It is about letting go of life. But most of all, it is about Death. The stories are their stories from the other side, and I am their storyteller. By Pam McCagh.Copy Wright

Memories from the Past.

Written Through Their Memories

This Book is Full of Beautiful Memories

It's about life; it's about Death and somewhere in between. Memories from the Past is about someone who gives up on life and then finds a reason to live again.

My books have taught me to understand and appreciate life and to understand and respect Death. I hope that there are many more stories to write. And I hope someone somewhere will find peace in one of their stories.

Reviewed by the American Readers' This Is A Must-Read Book! ©Pam McCagh. Copy Wright

Thank You
for Reading Their Book
And There Stories
Pam McCagh

Printed in Dunstable, United Kingdom